GEORGE CHAPMAN—THE EFFECT OF STOICISM UPON HIS TRAGEDIES

GEORGE CHAPMAN—THE EFFECT OF STOICISM UPON HIS TRAGEDIES

By John William Wieler

1969

OCTAGON BOOKS

New York

Reprinted 1969
by special arrangement with John William Wieler

OCTAGON BOOKS

A Division of Farrar, Straus & Giroux, Inc.
19 Union Square West
New York, N. Y. 10003

Library of Congress Catalog Card Number: 69-15235

Printed in U.S.A. by
NOBLE OFFSET PRINTERS, INC.
NEW YORK 3, N. Y.

FOR
MY MOTHER

PREFACE

ALTHOUGH George Chapman's indebtedness to the philosophy of Stoicism in *The Revenge of Bussy D'Ambois* and *The Tragedy of Caesar and Pompey* has long been recognized, scholars heretofore have limited their discussion of this influence to the importance it naturally assumes as a part of any general critical commentary. The extent to which Stoicism shaped the course of Chapman's development as a writer of dramatic tragedy has never become the subject of any one study. An opportunity therefore exists for a critical essay devoted entirely to an analysis of the effects of Stoic doctrine upon Chapman's art in tragedy, not only upon the two dramas in which Stoicism is most apparent, but also upon the tragedies comprising the entire canon.

It is hoped that this study may also be of some assistance in solving the problem of dating Chapman's last play. As the matter now stands, *The Tragedy of Chabot Admiral of France* is traditionally considered to have been the last of Chapman's tragedies, though the evidence is not altogether conclusive. Without being able to be any more conclusive, I have nevertheless suggested that there is some reason for believing that *The Tragedy of Caesar and Pompey* represents Chapman's last dramatic effort.

Of far greater interest and significance, however, is the new light that I trust this study of Chapman's indebtedness to the Stoic ethics throws upon the playwright's treatment of character and situation, particularly upon these provocative issues: why Chapman's development as a Stoic contributed to his failure as a dramatist and why the possibilities of so great a dramatist as Chapman were never realized.

I owe a debt of gratitude to many people who have given freely of their minds, time, and patience during the years in which this work was in progress. In particular, I extend hearty thanks to three members of the Department of English and Comparative Literature of Columbia University: to Professor Oscar James Campbell for his scholarly guidance and friendly counsel during all my Columbia years; to Professor Marjorie Hope Nicolson for her invaluable criticism, kindly faith, and work-compelling inspiration; and to Professor Emeritus Ernest Hunter Wright for his many helpful suggestions.

It is also a pleasure to record my indebtedness to three other members of the Columbia staff: to Mrs. Adele Mendelsohn, secretary of the Department of English, whose unfaltering kindness and friendship have served always to make my every goal seem possible of attainment; to Miss Jacqueline Castles and Miss Jean Macalister, of the Butler Library, whose eagerness to be of assistance has solved many problems.

To the Trustees of Columbia University, who granted me a University Fellowship for the completion of this work, I express my deepest gratitude.

Finally, I wish to thank three friends of long standing whose rich fellowship has eased my path in no small way on numerous occasions: Dr. Muriel Bowden, Dr. Grace Calder, and Mr. Eberhardt E. LeSchin.

J. W. W.

New York City
February, 1949

ACKNOWLEDGMENTS

FOR PERMISSION to use the copyrighted material in this volume, acknowledgement is made to the following publishers and authors: E. P. Dutton & Company, Inc., for passages from Thomas Marc Parrott's *The Comedies of George Chapman*, 1914, and *The Tragedies of George Chapman*, 1910; Harvard University Press, Loeb Classical Library, for passages from Cicero's *De Senectute, De Amicitia, De Divinatione*, translated by Walter Miller, 1928, from Plutarch's *Moralia*, Vols. II and IV, translated by Frank Cole Babbit, 1928-36, from Seneca's *Ad Lucilium Epistulae Morales*, translated by Richard M. Gummere, Vols. I, II, and III, 1925, 1930, 1925, and from Theodore Spencer's *Death and Elizabethan Tragedy*, 1936; D. C. Heath & Company, for a passage from *Bussy D'Ambois* and *The Revenge of Bussy D'Ambois*, 1905; The Johns Hopkins Press, for passages from *A Journal of English Literary History*, Vol. XII, No. 2 (1945), and *Modern Language Notes*, Vol. XLVIII (1933) and Vol. LIII (1938); Longmans, Green & Company, Inc., for passages from Eduard Zeller's *The Stoics, Epicureans and Sceptics*, translated by Rev. Oswald J. Reichel, 1892; Louisiana State University Press, for a passage from Howard Baker's *Induction to Tragedy*, 1939; Methuen & Company, Ltd., for a passage from "The Tragedy of Julius Caesar," *The Works of Shakespeare*, 1902; Modern Language Association, for passages from Phyllis Brooks Bartlett's *The Poems of George Chapman*, 1941; Oxford University Press, for passages from *Notes and Queries*, Vol. I, Series 12 (1916), and Vol. CLXIV (1933), from *Review of English Studies*, Vol. XIII (1937), from Hardin Craig's *The Enchanted Glass*, 1936, from H. Dugdale Sykes' *Sidelights on Elizabethan Drama*, London, 1924, and from Whitney J. Oates' *The Stoic and Epicurean Philosophers*, 1940; Principia Press, for passages from Laurens J. Mills' *One Soul in Bodies Twain*, 1937; the publishers of *Scrutiny*, for passages from Vol. III (1934-35) and Vol. IV (1935-36); University of California Press, for passages from Willard Farnham's *The Medieval Heritage of Elizabethan Tragedy*, 1936; University of Illinois Press, for passages from *Journal of English and Germanic Philology*, Vol. XXIX (1930); University of Michigan Press, for a passage from Norma D. Solve's *Stuart Politics in Chapman's "Tragedy of Chabot,"* 1928; University of Washington Press, for passages from *Modern Language Quarterly*, Vol. III (1942); University of Wisconsin Press, for passages from H. B. Lathrop's *Translations from the Classics into English from Caxton to Chapman, 1477-1620*, 1933.

CONTENTS

GEORGE CHAPMAN—THE EFFECT OF STOICISM UPON HIS TRAGEDIES

PROLOGUE

THE MANY editions of Marcus Aurelius, Cicero, Epictetus, Plutarch, and Seneca published during the time of the Renaissance indicate a growing interest in the philosophy of Stoicism, particularly in its ethics.[1] As early as 1567, for example, James Sanford introduced his edition of Epictetus' *Manual* as derived from "a large volume . . . than the which there cane be no Booke to the wel framing of our life more profitable and necessary."[2] It was inevitable in a period when the classics were coming to be regarded as a great storehouse of wisdom that the ethics of Stoicism should be adopted to support those of Christian thought which they so often paralleled. In his Preface to Guilaume DuVair's *The Moral Philosophie of the Stoics* Thomas James wrote in 1598:

> Let it not seeme strange vnto vs that Philosophie should be a meanes to help Diuinitie, or that Christians may profit by the Stoicks. Indeede the licentious loosenes of our times cannot well brooke the strictnes of this sect. . . . no kinde of philosophie is more profitable and neerer approching vnto Christiantie (as *S. Hierome* saith) than the philosophie of the Stoicks. Let vs then that are Christians follow them as farre foorth as they haue followed the trueth.[3]

Again, in his 1620 edition of Seneca's *Works,* Thomas Lodge advised the Reader, "What a Stoicke hath written, Reade thou like a Christian."[4] Recommendations such as these point to the strong influence exerted by Stoicism upon the thinking and writing of men of the Renaissance.

The problem of isolating Stoic doctrines in the literary work of any given writer is complicated, not so much by their closeness to Christian ideology, as by the fact that these doctrines are rarely adopted in their entirety. Just as the student can frequently detect influences of Christianity in an author's thinking simply because certain of its major tenets have become an integral part of the conventional patterns of most men's thinking, so the student often finds specific evidences of Stoicism in a writer of the Renaissance only to discover later that his "find" can be duplicated in the works of many authors. He must, therefore, come to the conclusion that a general knowledge of Stoicism was in the air, was indeed a part of the thinking of the man who moved in a world dominated by the prevalent ideas of his age; such evidence can never be conclusive. If, on the other hand, he finds an author whose knowledge of Stoicism transcends the conventional patterns of the age, who displays a familiarity with the distinguishing concepts of the philosophy, and who follows the thinking of Epictetus, for example, not merely as a mental exercise but as a philosophy of life, the student may then say without fear of contradiction: this poet, this playwright, was shaped by Stoic influences. George Chapman was such a man. Many of his occasional poems, particularly those written after 1611-12, reveal that to a great extent the poet's thinking was motivated by Stoic ideology. *Bussy D'Ambois* (1603-04), however, Chapman's first tragedy, reflects the dramatist's familiarity with only a few of the more common decrees of Stoicism; we shall, therefore, examine first those doctrines a knowledge of which indicates little more than the fact that Chapman was conversant with the popular ethics of Stoicism.

The pre-eminent position occupied by Reason in the whole corpus of Stoic philosophy was primarily due to its being identified with God. The close relationship between Reason and the Divine Being is attested by Seneca's statement that "reason . . . is nothing else than a portion of the divine spirit set in a human body."[5] Indoctrinated with a belief in the sacred origins of his reasoning faculty, the Stoical man revered this faculty of reason as a determinant for the rejection of impressions or judgments that might

interfere with the inner calm he persistently cultivated. Reason became the Stoic's moated castle, his refuge from the world, the one
place from which, while observing the scene about him, he could
attempt to fit all the parts of life's puzzle into a system that would
enable him to maintain almost with ease a calm acceptance of whatever befell him. Reason, then, became the source of his happiness[6]
as he lived in accord with God's will.

Having adopted the rational approach as a governing principle
for the individual's private life, the Stoics simply extended it to
include his public life as well, for, as Seneca writes, "If reason becomes your ruler, you will become ruler over many."[7] Had the
Stoics followed their own theory, they never could have become
statesmen who took an active part in the affairs of government; for
the highly personal character of their ethics suggested a relationship between the ruler and the ruled that amounted to little more
than maintaining the *status quo*. When Reason dictates that "it is a
bad soldier who grumbles when following his commander,"[8] man
can do nothing but accept the situation at hand; conformity rather
than reformation must be his policy.

The emphasis of the Stoic ethics upon Reason inevitably demanded that man must be wise. Epictetus himself told his students
at the Stoa, "All your attention must be given to the mind."[9] It
naturally followed that he who cultivated his mind became wise, an
attainment that Seneca urged when he wrote, "Our abiding-place
should be in wisdom itself."[10] All men, however, could not hope
to aspire to this state, for wisdom occupied in the Stoic philosophy
the absolute position described in Epictetus' words, "The quality
of *being wise* can fall to the lot of the good man alone."[11] The fact
that the good wise man alone merited attention and respect is
largely responsible for the Stoic insistence upon the individuality
of man, upon the self-sufficiency of his life.

The ethical implications of being wise as a Stoic, however, do not
remain wholly general in character; certain very practical consider-

ations control his actions at all times. Seneca learned through his relationship to Nero as tutor and later as adviser that the wise man could ill afford to incur the wrath of the ruler. Likewise, he found it impractical to "upset the customs of the people," to "invite the attention of the populace by any novel ways of living."[12] His opportunity for reforming the life of others being thus limited, the Stoical man of necessity remained largely preoccupied with the ethics of his own private life.

The concern of the Stoic ethics with the man of wisdom indicates clearly that Roman Stoicism had departed widely from Greek thinking. Whereas the Greeks devoted themselves to developing the natural nobility of all men, the Stoics of the Roman world confined themselves to those men with good minds who composed a select aristocracy. Their nobility, a society whose criterion was that of intellectual superiority, contained no place for the men whom Seneca disparagingly calls "the people" and "the populace."

Such an attitude was abetted by the Stoic conception of virtue, a stern reality, a positive quality that encompassed only the good and excluded all evil. Being "nothing else than right reason,"[13] virtue assumed something of the absolute quality of wisdom since it "needs nothing to set it off."[14] While it is true that Epictetus restricted both Plutarch's and Cicero's criticism of the absolutist conception of virtue when he stated, "If this is the promise that virtue makes to us—the promise to produce happiness and peace and calm, surely progress towards virtue is progress toward each of these,"[15] the focusing of attention on the wise man who embodies all virtues, who is himself an embodiment of the ideal of the highest good, remained an accepted doctrine of Stoic teaching.

That the virtuous wise man might better be able to maintain his reasoned calm, the Stoics attempted to free him from the influence of his emotions through the exercise of his reason. To them, all emotions were disturbing, whether of joy or of sorrow, for, as Seneca noted, "There is an equality between feeling joy with self-control and suffering pain with self-control,"[16] a self-control which Marcus Aurelius' insistence upon "no violent emotion"[17] serves to emphasize.

The distrust with which the Stoics regarded any domination of the senses accounts to some extent for their disdain of pleasure, that is, of *voluptas*. Cicero warns that "in pleasure's realm there is not a single spot where virtue can put her foot. . . . For carnal pleasure hinders deliberation, is at war with reason, blindfolds the eyes of the mind . . . and has no fellowship with virtue."[18] And Seneca's statement that "we are accustomed to use the word [pleasure] when we wish to indicate a happy state of mind"[19] is a further indication that joy or pleasure applies not to the senses or to any form of sensuality but to that imperturbability of mind and spirit to which the Stoic's life was so conscientiously devoted and with which the senses always interfere.

Similarly, Epictetus' belief that "one man cannot make another miserable"[20] accounts for the Stoic insistence that Reason must rule over grief. Plutarch praised a man as "sensible . . . who has made up his mind beforehand to conform uncomplainingly and obediently to the dispensation of things . . . Reason is the best remedy for the cure of grief, reason and the preparedness through reason for all the changes of life."[21]

Thus, by devitalizing the influence of the emotions upon man's life did the Stoics enable the reasoning faculty so to dominate him that it became a bulwark against anything that might happen to him. Man's mind was his citadel; peace of mind and the resulting tranquility of spirit constituted much of his happiness.

Living according to Nature was another ethical principle that often directed the Stoic's quest for mental peace. Just what did he understand the words to mean? It is the Epictetus of the *Discourses* who conveniently answers the question: "What do you mean by 'nature'? I mean, God's will."[22] This answer gives to Nature a meaning somewhat different from any we are accustomed to use.

Explicit in the term is the idea of an original and rational force that at all times directs both the universe and man himself, as if God were everywhere at work that all things might proceed according to a preconceived plan. And man's obligation to God's will represents the ethical substance of the Stoic principle of conforming to Nature's laws.

That the idea of Nature embodied a fixed goal is also revealed in the *Manual:* "For nature mother of all things, hath framed every man to some particular thing."[23] Each man, then, has within him a destiny to be fulfilled, no matter what emphasis he places upon solving the problem of the moment; that destiny is closely allied with the doctrine of living according to Nature. Furthermore, the corollary follows that each man can successfully chart his own course of action since he knows what he must do and what he must not do. It is, therefore, possible for the Stoical man to maintain control over every situation which arises to confront him. He can shape his life to conform both to his destiny and to his own satisfaction as well.[24]

The reliance of the Stoic philosophers on the reasoning faculty helps to explain their contempt for the Goddess Fortuna, as popular in medieval literature as in the Greek classics. If they accepted her fanciful whims, they had to renounce their unruffled calm, achieved through rational precepts. Epictetus himself states that the Stoic's happiness derives from his banishment of Fortune as an active force upon his mental life: "The ideal man, whom we have snatched from the control of the people and of Fortune, is happy inwardly."[25] Nor would the Stoics permit man to attribute to Fortune his own errors at the sacrifice of his own resilience to her fancies: "It is we ourselves who have attributed our own misdeeds to Fortune. . . . For these two things are, as it were, at opposite poles—good fortune and good heart; that is why we are wiser when in the midst of adversity."[26] The defiance with which the Stoic faced Fortune left him no alternative except to give himself over completely to Destiny.

A final resignation to Destiny, the end shaped for him at his birth from which there can be no escape, as opposed to Fortune, the erratic Goddess who presides over the chance happenings of both good and evil in man's life, was the Stoic's only salvation if he were to remain indifferent to the vicissitudes of life. His reason demanded that he accept the principle set forth by Marcus Aurelius: "Love that only which happens to thee and is spun with the thread of thy destiny. . . . Whatever may happen to thee, it was prepared for thee from all eternity; and the implication of causes was from eternity spinning the thread of thy being, and of that which is incident to it."[27]

The doctrines thus far reviewed must represent the common denominator of Stoicism, the conventional ideas which we have every reason to believe pervaded the thinking and writing of the sixteenth century, as of succeeding centuries. If they represented the full impact of the Stoic philosophy on the development of Chapman as a writer of dramatic tragedy, we should have to conclude that the influence upon the artist had been negligible. Indeed, in his first tragedy, *Bussy D'Ambois,* we shall find that Chapman's art was little affected by even the more obvious and well-known dicta of Stoicism. Evidences of Stoic influence are certainly apparent in *Bussy;* however, this play, which dramatic criticism has almost unanimously given first place among all his tragedies, remains remarkably untouched by the very fundamentals of Stoic ethics.

Though scholars have rarely judged that any other of the five tragedies in the Chapman canon equals *Bussy* in dramatic power, they have been quick to note that in at least two of these plays, *The Revenge of Bussy D'Ambois* and *The Tragedy of Caesar and Pompey,* Chapman reveals a thoroughgoing comprehension of Stoic doctrines. A careful reading of the Roman Stoics and of the

Chapman tragedies which followed *Bussy* indicates that the author was becoming more and more conversant with the whole range of Stoic principles of conduct and decorum. No longer does Chapman reflect only a general knowledge of Stoicism, a knowledge which any cultured man of his day might be expected to possess. He has now become a student of those less conventional and more provocative tenets, so often peculiar to Stoicism alone, to such an extent that his artistry in tragedy is noticeably affected. That we may evaluate the extent and nature of this influence, we must examine other Stoic beliefs that Chapman obviously knew and was coming to accept.

Though the Stoic philosophers schooled their followers to rely primarily upon Reason for the attainment of mental peace, they nevertheless sought to strengthen their ethical position with doctrines that would protect the Stoic from dissatisfaction with his worldly lot. Learning to accept the world as he found it, remaining content with things as they were and not as he might wish them to be, became one of his deepest satisfactions. Epictetus' injunction, "Ask not that events should happen as you will, but let your will be that events should happen as they do, and you shall have peace,"[28] accounts for the spirit of resignation which the Stoic writers advocate again and again if man is to achieve peace of mind. They saw no other way of combating the fickleness of Fortune and a world seemingly ruled by chance than to ignore everything that might disrupt the Stoic's equilibrium, and ignoring the world became synonymous with resigning oneself to it. Seneca expressed the idea in terms of man's everyday life, giving it a practical application: "When everything seems to go hard and uphill, I have trained myself not merely to obey God, but to agree with His decisions. . . . Nothing will ever happen to me that I shall receive with ill humour or with a wry face."[29]

The Stoics' refusal to be influenced by external events was dictated by Reason. Epictetus saw the problem clearly: "If you want outward things, let your reason go, or you will have neither the one nor the other, being pulled both ways."[30] If man was to maintain his inner peace, he had to be willing to discard everything that promised to destroy it: "We must give up our body, and all that belongs to it—faculties, property, reputation, offices, honours, children, brothers, friends—all these we must regard as having no concern for us."[31] The good Stoic, then, was faced—in theory, if not in practice—with the necessity of denying any ambition he might entertain of assuming an active part in the affairs of government since the implication is clear that such an aspiration would be dangerous, would lack virtue. Certainly the Stoics withheld their approval of the man whose greatness derived from material advantages. But they were eager to acclaim the man whose goodness heralded the contentment of his inner being.

Despite the fact that Epictetus classed "friends" among those externals man must forego as none of his concern, a Stoic maintained at the level of intellectual superiority a high regard for the concept of friendship. Cicero makes the point very clearly in his *De Amicitia:* "I am inclined to think that, with the exception of wisdom, no better thing has been given to man by the immortal gods."[32] But the Stoical man did not renounce his security attained through Reason for the sake of friends; he did not acknowledge any sense of need for them, believing rather that friendship is "cultivated by those who are most abundantly blessed with wealth and power and especially with virtue, which is man's best defense; by those least in need of another's help; and by those most generous and most given to acts of kindness."[33] Of all Stoic doctrines, that of friendship seems least affected by the demands of Stoic practicality. Nor is there any indication that friendship is to be considered lightly. It appears at all times as one of the strongest forces at work in the Stoic's life, for, more than any other tenet of his philosophy, it caused him to turn his eyes away from himself toward another, albeit one like himself.

The emphasis among the Stoics upon the completely masculine character of friendship is fundamental. While this predominantly male tone may suggest abnormality to the student familiar with the classical attitude toward homosexuality, yet the honesty with which the Stoics looked at both their world and themselves makes necessary no other explanation of the friendship between members of their exclusively male sect than that of their peculiar mental interests. Stoicism, indeed all classical antiquity, excluded women from the life of the mind. Epictetus even goes so far as to suggest that marriage and Stoicism are incompatible[34] since family ties may lead to disquietude. A partnership that amounted to a marriage of the minds of good men exposed a man to no such calamity.

When the Stoic philosophers had described the essential character of the ideal Stoic's life, they turned their attention to death, for which Reason dictated the same preparation of the mind as for life. Man must "be able to depart from life contentedly."[35] Such a belief minimized the importance of death, which had for the Stoics the finality of an eternal end, and emphasized the opinion "that not the longest life is the best, but the most efficient."[36] With efficiency rather than long life the criterion of successful living, the Stoic was at all times faced with a philosophy of life that relegated the "hereafter" to a position of no great concern to him. Thoughts of a death that promised him nothing simply made him more devoted to a life that both promised and provided the only happiness he knew. In facing death, he continued to demonstrate his invulnerability to anything over which his reason could rule.

In one of his references to death, Seneca writes, "In other years time did not seem to me to go so swiftly; now, it seems fast beyond belief, perhaps because I feel that the finish-line is moving closer to me, or it may be that I have begun to take heed and reckon up my losses."[37] It was this very reckoning up of losses that led the Stoics to condone suicide when Reason approved it. Epictetus expresses the idea in an extreme form: "When a man comes to feel that it is rational, he goes out and hangs himself at once."[38] Seneca also emphasizes the fact that Reason must be the final authority for suicide: "Reason, too, advises us to die . . . according to our ability, and to seize upon whatever means shall offer itself for doing violence to ourselves."[39] Neither of these statements, however, was meant to be taken as a kind of wholesale license for doing away with oneself; the Stoics held that within the bounds of Reason, suicide was to be chosen only by certain people faced with several clearly defined situations. Among these, old age received specific attention.

Seneca regarded old age as a state to be endured only if man retained those faculties which had made younger years happy ones: "I shall not abandon old age, if old age preserves me intact for myself . . . but if old age begins to shatter my mind, and to pull its various faculties to pieces, if it leaves me, not life, but only the breath of life, I shall rush out of a house that is crumbling and tottering."[40] Similarly, only an illness that is incurable justifies suicide:

> I shall not avoid illness by seeking death, as long as the illness is curable and does not impede my soul. I shall not lay violent hands upon myself just because I am in pain; for death under such circumstances is defeat. But if I find out that the pain must always be endured, I shall depart, not because of the pain, but because it will be a hindrance to me as regards all my reasons for living. He who dies just because he is in pain is a weakling, a coward; but he who lives merely to brave out this pain, is a fool.[41]

The Stoics, then, regarded any phase of life—old age or an incurable illness—over which man had failed to maintain control as lost to him. The possibility of such a loss was not to be tolerated, for it seriously interfered with the Stoic's strong belief that the complete control of his inner calm was in his own hands at all times.

But if suicide had been permitted the Stoic only when he was the victim of a crumbling old age or of an uncontrollable illness, this aspect of his ethics could never have achieved great prominence. It remained for Cicero to impose suicide upon certain men as a duty under particular circumstances:

> Diversity of character carries with it so great significance that suicide may be for one man a duty, for another [under the same circumstances] a crime. Did Marcus Cato find himself in one predicament, and were the others, who surrendered to Caesar in Africa, in another? And yet, perhaps, they would have been condemned, if they had taken their lives; for their mode of life had been less austere and their characters more pliable. But Cato had been endowed by nature with an austerity beyond belief, and he himself had strengthened it by unswerving consistency and had remained ever true to his purpose and fixed resolve; and it was for him to die rather than to look upon the face of a tyrant.[42]

It is this possibilty of suicide for those whom tyranny would force to abandon their Stoical principles of living that made the greatest appeal, for, when suicide becomes the duty of the man who has lost control of the conditions under which he must live, then the decision for self-slaughter has been reduced to a debate between Reason and circumstance; Reason must carry the decision.

Stoicism appealed to men of the Renaissance at these two levels, the general and the specific, both of which helped to shape the course of literary history. The former permeated the intellectual life of the period; the latter, though obviously less well known, made the more important contribution. Both are to be found in the tragedies of George Chapman. A careful reading of Chapman's tragedies reveals, not only that his knowledge of Stoicism existed

on these two planes, but also that the influence that they exerted
varied sharply as the dramatist progressed from the conventional
level to that embodying the more sober philosophical tenets. It is
conceivable that a playwright who manipulated tragic situations
and characters according to thoroughly rational principles of virtuous conduct divorced from the impulses of emotional reactions
might produce a tragedy devoid of the conflict that is the essence of
all drama. But no such principle obtained when Chapman wrote
Bussy D'Ambois, and the play emerges as a highly successful example of Renaissance tragedy. Stoicism has not as yet affected the
author's artistry to any marked extent.

It is not conceivable, however, that any playwright could create
from those Stoic doctrines that comprise the more impressive con-
tributions of the philosophy a successful and impelling tragedy.
Learning to accept the world as one finds it, for example, is a principle of conduct that no doubt greatly aided the Stoic in his quest
for happiness. But just as certainly any such studied defense of
passivity to the forces of life in the range of human experience
lacks dramatic *élan.* Even more than a strict rationalism, such a doctrine vitiates a man's inclination to rebel, for resignation does not
foster that kind of conflict in which dramatic tragedy especially
must find its power. Such power can never spring from the Stoic's
acquiescence in an ethics that regards all struggle as futile. Again, a
man may develop a feeling of self-sufficiency by refusing to grant
importance to outward greatness in favor of his own inner goodness; yet no life could be more static, less deficient in dramatic
vitality, less instinct with tragic possibility, than the Stoic's satisfaction with his "unruffled inward peace."[43]

In terms of the theatre, the Stoic concept of a male friendship is
equally devoid of dramatic potentiality, for its identity with the
Stoic's inner life and mind continued to restrict his opportunity for
active association with men of that external world to whom he refused his intimate fellowship. A world peopled entirely by Stoic

men only guarantees the equilibrium of the individual life. Nor does the absence of women tend to enliven the scene. Secure though the Stoic may have found a life confined to the quietness of the mind, the limitations under which it was achieved resulted in a kind of monotony that the nature of his friendships did little but re-enforce.

Moreover, the Stoic's contempt for death and his readiness to elect suicide when he is no longer capable of directing his own course fails at all times to give his life a semblance of tragic significance. Such an attitude may on occasion assume a certain theatricality, but it can never attain the nobility of that tragedy in which a figure of heroic stature forestalls rather than invites his own destruction. Great tragic heroes like Oedipus and Macbeth command attention again and again because their will to live refuses to succumb to the disaster that threatens to overwhelm them.

And yet these very principles of conduct represent the Stoic influences at work upon Chapman as he wrote *The Revenge of Bussy D'Ambois, The Tragedy of Chabot Admiral of France,* and *The Tragedy of Caesar and Pompey.* They do not all appear full-blown at the outset, for Stoicism continued as a living and growing force upon Chapman's art until finally the artist and the philosophy of Stoicism often seemed to become one. It was therefore no accident that no one of these later tragedies met with the success of *Bussy;* as Stoicism became with him a real philosophy of life, his artistry in handling tragic effects exhibits a corresponding decline. Chapman's devotion to Stoic ethics hinders rather than enhances his tragic style.

As Chapman passes from the conventional knowledge of the Stoicism so popular in the Renaissance to a more serious interest in this philosophy, then, he presents to the student of literary history several opportunities for the re-evaluation of his art in tragedy. In the first place, it becomes possible either to establish more firmly the accepted chronology of Chapman's tragedies or to suggest cer-

tain changes which seem more in accord with the author's development. More important, however, if it can be demonstrated that a
real correlation exists between the adoption of Stoicism as a way of
life and the decline of Chapman's tragic power, it follows that too
close an adaptation of Stoicism for dramatic purposes must lead to
the negation of tragedy.

THE TRAGEDIES

CHAPTER ONE: BUSSY D'AMBOIS

Muses that Fames loose feathers beautifie,
And such as scorne to tread the Theater,
As ignorant: the seede of memorie
Haue most inspirde, and showne theyr glories there
To noblest wits, and men of highest doome,
That for the kingly Lawrell bent affayre:
The Theaters of *Athens* and of *Rome*
Haue beene the Crownes, and not the base empayre.
Farre then be this foule clowdy-browd contempt
From like-plumde Birds: and let your sacred rymes
From honors Court theyr seruile feete exempt
That liue by soothing moods, and seruing tymes:
And let my loue, adorne with modest eyes,
Muses that sing loues sensuall emperyes.

From Chapman's "A Coronet for His Mistresse
Philosophie," Ovids Banqvet of Sence (1595).

THE DATE of composition of *Bussy D'Ambois,* Chapman's first known departure from dramatic comedy, presents interesting problems to the student attracted by the author's concern with Stoicism. According to Professor Parrott, this play was "composed for the Children of the Chapel shortly after the death of Elizabeth, and in 1603 or 1604 was carried over in MS.—perhaps before it had been acted—to the rival company of boy actors, the Children of Paul's, by whom it was, as the title-page of the first edition [1607] tells us, 'often presented.' "[1] The date of 1603 or 1604 places the first writing of *Bussy* not far distant from the time of composition of the comedy *Sir Giles Goosecap,* "the autumn of 1601 . . . and the early spring of 1603";[2] and it is in *Sir Giles* that the "singularly cold-blooded and ratiocinative lover,"[3] Clarence, appears. Of him Professor Parrott writes, "M. Schoell does not go too far, I think, in saying that the philosophy of Clarence contains in the germ, at least, almost all the tenets of Chapman's later philosophy."[4] We may expect to find, then, further indications of Chapman's interest in Stoicism in *Bussy* when Chapman turns his attention to tragedy. And while Miss Bartlett's statement that Hieronymus Wolfius' translation of Epictetus "was Chapman's most important reading in the years 1611-12"[5] applies most significantly to a study of *The Revenge of Bussy D'Ambois,* we must not lose sight of the fact that *Bussy* was revised at a time when Chapman's thinking was being affected by the Stoic philosophers. Though the date of the revision, which Parrott considers to be about 1610,[6] does not fall within the time when Chapman's thinking was known to have been affected most by Epictetus, yet evidence within the play itself indicates that Chapman was indebted to Seneca, Plutarch, and Erasmus, upon whom he leaned heavily in all his work. The reading of Epictetus may have served later to bring his thinking into sharper focus, but the philosophy of Stoicism was by no means new to Chapman when he was writing *Bussy,* especially the revised version. The revising of this play, if done in 1610, would bring this first of his tragedies into the same period as the others with which his mind was occupied for some six or seven years. After *The Conspiracy and Tragedy of Charles Duke of Byron,* composed "late in 1607 or early in 1608,"[7] came the revised *Bussy* in 1610; *The Revenge of Bussy D'Ambois,* "in 1610 or in 1611";[8] *The Tragedy of Caesar and Pompey,* "in 1612-13";[9] and *The Tragedy of Chabot Admiral of France,* between 1611 and 1624.[10] With the exception of the date of 1624, accepted in this study with qualification, the tragedies fall within the years from 1607 to 1613.

Heretofore, scholarship treating Chapman's interest in Stoicism has confined itself almost wholly to *The Revenge of Bussy* and to *Caesar and Pompey,* with Clermont, Chapman's "Senecal man" of the former play, the focus of attention. In these two plays and in this one character Stoical influences are certainly substantial, yet they had become manifest as early as 1603-04 when the playwright first turned from comedy to tragedy, a change in dramatic intent for which the Stoic ethics was largely responsible. Chapman might look upon Homer as another great teacher whom his world could ill afford to ignore, but he could express neither through his translation of *The Iliad* and *The Odyssey* nor through his minor poems his full preoccupation with the behavior of man. Drama was the only literary form remaining to him, a form which Chapman had already employed with great popular success[11] in the presentation of his comedies. He must have realized, however, that comedy is hardly an adequate medium in which to explore problems of conduct based on philosophical concepts. *Sir Giles Goosecap, Knight* illustrates this infelicity. When the tomfooleries of Sir Giles, Sir Cuthbert Rudesby, and Sir Clement Kingcob together with the "lady virgins and companions to Eugenia," Hippolyta and Penelope, are interrupted for the more serious talk of Eugenia, her uncle Momford, and Clarence, the play virtually stops while we are compelled to listen to a discussion, albeit interesting, of a cure for Clarence's lovesick soul. It may be argued that tragedy no more than comedy is a fit medium for such exposition, but certainly tragedy is better suited than comedy to a consideration of highly ethical issues. At the time when ethics was demanding more and more of Chapman's literary attention, it was to dramatic tragedy that he turned. *Bussy D'Ambois* was the result.

The *Epilogue* of 1641 opened with these lines:

> With many hands you have seen D'Ambois slain,
> Yet by your grace he may revive again,
> And every day grow stronger in his skill
> To please, as we presume he is in will.

If this passage had appeared in the first edition of 1607 or in the reissue of 1608,[12] the problem of interpreting *Bussy D'Ambois* in relation to *The Revenge* would be more simple. The Epilogue was probably spoken for the first time in the presentation of the 1610 revision; if so, this most important of changes must then have served as a promise to the audience that their favorite character might again tread the boards—"Yet by your grace he may revive again"; now it is an indication that *The Revenge* was germinating in Chapman's mind. For this sequel was forged from the conclusions of *Bussy D'Ambois,* was in fact created to act as its foil.

After Chapman had chosen his subject matter from French history, he had yet to select and motivate incidents suited to drama. The jealousy of Montsurry directed the action and gave *Bussy D'Ambois* the characteristics of the conventional revenge-tragedy. Because in 1603-04, when the play was first acted, the revenge-tragedy was at the height of its popularity, it must have been regarded by the audience as another play of a long line in which a typical Renaissance hero played the role of passion's slave. Combining the traditional features of this genre with themes of Fortune, Destiny, or Nature, the play became one of the most popular tragedies of Chapman, adding significance to his already well-established reputation as one of the leading writers of tragedy.[13]

Since Professor Parrott has been unable to note any source for *Bussy* "which attributes his death to Monsieur's jealousy and thwarted passion for Monsoreau's wife,"[14] we must accept the revenge theme in part "as representing, at least, a tradition familiar to Chapman."[15] This tradition, originating in English dramatic literature with Sackville and Kyd, was long attributed by scholars to the influence of Seneca. Recent scholars, however, tend to minimize this influence almost out of existence. Baker, for example, writes,

> We have very good reasons to believe that Seneca contributed rhetorical patches and practically nothing more; certainly nothing tangible to the form of the English tragedy; certainly nothing worth mentioning to its philosophy. Seneca, finally, like Machiavelli, seems to have been dragged by main force into modern criticism because he is a convenient peg on which to hang the disorderly and disintegrating materials

which the Sackvilles and the Kyds could not quite straighten out.[16]

Lathrop shares Baker's view: "It is also maintained that the violence, the bloodshed, the terror, and the descriptive element of English tragedy owes much to Seneca. To my mind, this credits too much to the Latin writer,"[17] On the other hand, Eliot holds that "Chapman uses him [Seneca], and employs the old machinery; but Seneca's influence on Chapman was chiefly on Chapman's 'thought', "[18] while Lucas believes that "as usual in Chapman, though he borrows Senecan mannerisms, his matter is his own."[19] Baker and Lathrop are probably right, for in this particular *Bussy* play, the absence of a known source to account for the springing of the revenge theme from Monsieur's and Montsurry's jealous passion does not make it necessary to attribute the action to Senecan or any other influence. The reason for jealousy and revenge is inherent as an active motivating force of the tragedy, and it seems unnecessary to fall back upon what has always passed for a dramatic tradition to explain a tragedy the cause of which is as old as mankind itself. And the more widely one reads in Elizabethan dramatic literature, the more obvious becomes the medieval and native heritage of English tragedy. Certainly there is little need to look further afield to account for Chapman's use of the revenge theme. The Fortune-tragedy, for example, which *Bussy* purports at the outset to be, is as old as medieval drama, having its roots deep in Boethius. That even the "matter" with which Chapman dresses the form "is his own" seems unlikely; not an original thinker, he borrowed in all his work from whatever source suited his purpose best and used that material as his own. Yet the Senecan theory ought no more to explain the avenging of the adultery of Tamyra and Bussy than to account for the avenging of Othello's supposedly violated honor.

Aside from Bussy himself, Tamyra is the only other character in this tragedy who completely reveals Chapman's artistry. Hers is the sole feminine portrait in all the tragedies that fully achieves life stature despite the fact that the dramatist, like his Stoic teachers, displays a lack of sympathy for womankind.[20] Tamyra's fault lies, however, not so much in her being a woman as in her failure as a woman to control her emotions. This weakness, responsible for Bussy's downfall as well as her own, represents to Chapman's mind, already inclined toward Stoic doctrine, his condemnation of the individual who becomes passion's slave—the human fault, which, as we shall see later, is also Bussy's tragic flaw. Tamyra remains a woman whom Reason cannot reform.

As the persons most injured by Tamyra's adultery with Bussy, both Monsieur and Montsurry direct much of their contempt for woman at her often violated chastity, and their remarks are an interesting composite, reflecting the vagaries of Cynthia, so common in sixteenth-century literature, and Stoic contempt for carnal pleasure. Montsurry almost disbelieves his wife's waywardness: "'Tis miraculous to think with what monsters women's imaginations engross them when they are once enamoured, and what wonders they will work for their satisfaction. They will make a sheep valiant, a lion fearful."[21] Monsieur re-echoes this weakness in woman's psychology:

> O the unsounded sea of women's bloods,
> That when 'tis calmest, is most dangerous! . . .
> Not Cerberus ever saw the damned nooks
> Hid with the veils of women's virtuous looks.[22]

Bussy's opinion of the nature of women is, however, nearer that of the sixteenth century than either Monsieur's or Montsurry's. He refutes Monsieur's earlier statement that men rule in women:

> So women, that (of all things made of nothing)
> Are the most perfect idols of the moon,
> (Or still-unwean'd sweet moon-calves with white faces)

Not only are patterns of change to men,
But, as the tender moonshine of their beauties
Clears or is cloudy, make men glad or sad:
So then they rule in men, not men in them.[23]

In a similar vein, Monsieur once comments to Montsurry, "Your
wife, you know is a mere Cynthia."[24] More in the classical and
Stoic vein is Montsurry's refusal at the height of his anger to entertain either the Friar's excuses or her own. When Tamyra suggests
that the "hereafter" may make her husband more kindly disposed
toward her "fault," Montsurry scoffs,

Hereafter? *'Tis a suppos'd infinite,*
That from this point will rise eternally:
Fame grows in going; *in the scapes of virtue*
Excuses damn her: they be fires in cities
Enrag'd with those winds that less lights extinguish.
Come, Siren, sing, and dash against my rocks
Thy ruffian galley, rigg'd with quench for lust![25]

He places the blame squarely on Tamyra, denouncing

The errant wilderness of a woman's face,
Where men cannot get out, for all the comets
That have been lighted at it: though they know
That adders lie a-sunning in their smiles
That basilisks drink their poison from their eyes,
And no way there to coast out to their hearts;[26]

and absolving men completely:

No man can add height to a woman's sin.
Vice never doth her just hate so provoke,
As when she rageth under virtue's cloak.[27]

And although Tamyra does not die at his hands, Montsurry reminds us of Othello, who held his honor more dear than Desdemona herself, when he replies to Tamyra's plea:

> I do forgive thee, and upon my knees,
> With hands held up to heaven, wish that mine honour
> Would suffer reconcilement to my love;
> But since it will not, honour never serve
> My love with flourishing object, till it sterve![28]

The portrait of Tamyra, though adverse in its criticism, is perhaps one of the best in all Chapman's tragedies from a dramatic viewpoint. Here is a woman plotting her own doom through unbridled and unreasoned passion, yet tortured at times by conscience and remorse because she cannot slough off the realization that her actions make her morally culpable. Bussy can ply her to his will, but he cannot make of Tamyra a partner blind to their sin; it is noteworthy that Tamyra herself stamps her actions as sinful. Though she can hardly be called Stoical, she is never morally unaware of her own ethical problem. We must agree with Boas that Tamyra appeals to us "because we see in her more of the conflict between passion and moral obligation, which is the essence of drama."[29] And because she is depicted as a person who can "clearly distinguish between virtue and nature,"[30] she is dramatically suited to Bussy, who remains incapable of making any such reasonable distinction and can, therefore, choose no worthy goal.

For, from the time Monsieur launches him upon his rise on Fortune's Wheel, Bussy seldom achieves the heroic stature that truly great tragic heroes attain. The noble words of the tragedy are rarely matched by comparable actions. Monsieur gives us the first clue to what we may expect in the character of Bussy:

> A man of spirit beyond the reach of fear,
> Who (discontent with his neglected worth)
> Neglects the light, and loves obscure abodes;

But he is young and haughty, apt to take
Fire at advancement, to bear state, and flourish.[31]

These lines must suggest that he is to be a tragic character who becomes lost in actions; yet his tragic significance rests largely on what
other characters have to say about him rather than upon what he
does to convince the reader of his right to any such claim. Bussy
himself would have us believe that Monsieur's craftiness is to conflict with his own knowledge that "virtuous deeds" must be the
salvation of the great man:

We must to Virtue for her guide resort,
Or we shall shipwrack in our safest port.[32]

Monsieur employs the same concept to persuade Bussy to enter his
service:

for as the light
Not only serves to show, but renders us
Mutually profitable, so our lives
In acts exemplary not only win
Ourselves good names, but do to others give
Matter for virtuous deeds, by which we live.[33]

But in spite of his fully expressed contempt for the "enchanted
glass"[34] of Court life, Bussy finally yields to Monsieur's persuasive
crowns, and soothes his conscience, saying,

I am for honest actions, not for great:
If I may bring up a new fashion,
And rise in Court for virtue, speed his [Monsieur's] plow![35]

In words, at least, Bussy may be said to have established his reputation for virtue, one of the attributes of the complete man,[36] but we
shall search in vain within the play for substantiating actions.

Bussy's boldness in both word and deed is another of his salient
characteristics. This boldness knows no bounds, being as much a

part of Bussy's manner with kings as with servants, with men as with women. It is his brusque and impudent manner with Maffé in the first scene of Act I that causes Monsieur's steward to exclaim, "These crowns are set in blood; blood be their fruit!"[37] when Bussy strikes him with the impetuosity so typical of both the man and the play. Again, on the occasion of his first appearance before the King and his Court, Bussy's lack of modesty causes the Duchess to remark, "He is much guilty of the bold extre/mity."[38] The Guise, resentful of the attention Bussy gives to his Duchess, upbraids him with the remark, "Go to, companion, your courtship's too saucy,"[39] a remark which serves only to make Bussy persist in those attentions. And when Monsieur later urges him to "leave courting his wife, then,"[40] Bussy's refusal and domination of the scene lead Monsieur to comment:

> [*Aside*] His great heart will not down, 'tis like the sea,
>   That partly by his own internal heat,
>   Partly the stars' daily and nightly motion,
>   Their heat and light, and partly of the place
>   The divers frames, but chiefly by the moon,
>   Bristled with surges, never will be won,
>   (No, not when th' hearts of all those powers are
>   burst)
>   To make retreat into his settled home,
>   Till he be crown'd with his own quiet foam.[41]

Here are lines of true poetic quality with a well-turned simile, but what is there in the action to call them forth or to warrant their sentiment? Is a man to be raised to great heights because he has the audacity to court another's wife in public with fine scorn for the husband? Were some momentous issue the reason for this poetic outburst, we might accept it with greater credulity; as it is, however, the link between the action and the judgment we are asked to

accept is missing, for the action and the words are incompatible—
their disparity striking, both morally and artistically.

The same criticism of this Renaissance hero also obtains after
Monsieur and Bussy have successfully persuaded the King to condone Bussy's killing of the three whose "fleerings" from the side-
lines aroused Bussy's "jealousy." Monsieur argues that

> Manly slaughter
> Should never bear th'account of wilful murther;[42]

that his

> friend only sav'd his fame's dear life,
> Which is above life, taking th'under value,
> Which, in the wrong it did, was forfeit to him;
> And in this fact only preserves a man
> In his uprightness, worthy to survive
> Millions of such as murther men alive.[43]

After Henry has yielded to this entreaty of Monsieur, Bussy is left
free to utter his own opinion of God and Nature at work in him,
concluding with the lines which exalt his own individuality:

> Who to himself is law, no law doth need,
> Offends no law, and is a king indeed.[44]

The student of Chapman recognizes this sentiment as one lodged
deep in Chapman's mind and often stated. But here, as in other instances, the question of artistic propriety arises: has Chapman
through Bussy succeeded in justifying murder by means of this
highly idealized conception of the law of the individual? If we
agree that he has not, another question then demands consideration: was Chapman creating in this tragedy a portrait of the man of
action in which he did not necessarily believe, but which was to
serve him later as a foil and contrast for such men of reflection as
Clermont, Chabot, and Cato? In such a problem, what Chapman

found in his source materials is of little consequence, for rarely in the history of the drama does the source dictate the treatment of materials: if the detail fits the author's purpose, it is taken over, often times *in toto;* if it does not, it is either omitted or changed for the purpose at hand. We shall return later to a consideration of Bussy as the antithesis of his more thoughtful brethren.

Chapman develops the portrait of the irresponsible, impetuous, valiant, and virtuous Bussy with many similar strokes. Typical is the Guise's taunting of Bussy with the fact that he is a bastard. Bussy retorts:

> Still shall we chide and foam upon this bit?
> Is the Guise only great in faction?
> Stands he not by himself? Proves he th' opinion
> That men's souls are without them? Be a duke,
> And lead me to the field.[45]

The Guise is willing to fight, but Henry stops the intended duel, and goes on to praise Bussy:

> Stay them! Stay, D'Ambois! Cousin Guise, I wonder
> Your honour'd disposition brooks so ill
> A man so good, that only would uphold
> Man in his native noblesse, from whose fall
> All our dissensions rise; that in himself
> (Without the outward patches of our frailty,
> Riches and honour) knows he comprehends
> Worth with the greatest: kings had never borne
> Such boundless empire over other men,
> Had all maintain'd the spirit and state of D'Ambois.[46]

And again the reader cannot help wondering at the glaring disparity between the action, if such it may be called, and the judgment of it. At the base of the whole argument we have Bussy's guilt with Tamyra which he refuses to regard as a sin, but which we are forced to consider in forming our conception of the man's character; we go on to his denunciation of men whose guilt appears to be of no greater degree than his; and we arrive finally at Henry's defense of the bastard that raises him "in his native noblesse" to a position comparable with that of "the noble savage," all the time lacking, however, a valid, ethical reason for the conclusion that Henry draws. We are simply asked to accept it as his conclusion.

In fact, the only evidence at all contradictory to the Umbra Friar's evaluation of Bussy after his death, "Farewell, brave relics of a complete man,"[47] occurs in the scene between Bussy and Monsieur when the two give themselves over to a thoroughgoing, penetrating "dissection" of each other. Then and then only do we get a view of Bussy that is complete, one in which all the characteristics previously given are tempered by contrasts—he is daring, headstrong, bloody, valourous, soulless, childish, villainous, ridiculous, vainglorious, impudent, prideful, a hackster, slave, murderer, mad quarreler, of vinegar-heart and toad-pool in complexion[48]—a man who

> in those humours wouldst envy, betray,
> Slander, blaspheme, change each hour a religion,[49]

and who studies

> calumnies and treacheries,
> To thy friends' slaughters like a screech-owl sing,
> And to all mischiefs, but to kill the King.[50]

Only at the time of his death does Bussy achieve that unanimity of word and deed that marks him as a man both in his own mind and in ours:

> let my death
> Define life nothing but a courtier's breath.
> Nothing is made of nought, of all things made,
> Their abstract being a dream but of a shade.
> I'll not complain to earth yet, but to heaven,
> And, like a man, look upwards even in death.

And if Vespasian thought in majesty
An emperor might die standing, why not I?
                She offers to help him
Nay, without help, in which I will exceed him;
For he died splinted with his chamber grooms.
Prop me, true sword, as thou hast ever done!
The equal thought I bear of life and death
Shall make me faint on no side; I am up;
Here like a Roman statue I will stand
Till death hath made me marble. *Oh, my fame,*
Live in despite of murther! Take thy wings . . .
Fly . . .
And tell them all that D'Ambois now is hasting
To the eternal dwellers; that a thunder
Of all their sighs together (for their frailties
Beheld in me) may quit my worthless fall
With a fit volley for my funeral.[51]

Bussy dies a Stoic death in the popular understanding of the word
—with proper respect for Destiny, without fear for what lies ahead
—requesting forgiveness from his murderers, minimizing for the
first time his own worth, and also achieving for the first time,
strangely enough, a balance between his actions and his appraisal
of them.

Hardin Craig counsels students that "the important thing is to
search the mind of the Renaissance in order to discover, not what
we of the current world believe is true, but what the poets and the
literary men of the Renaissance believed was true." Consequently,
the student who would understand Chapman must realize that the
dramatist "enters into the very centre of the realm of mental and
emotional life, making his entry through the portals of what were
to him the sciences of psychology and ethics."[52] These statements
are of the utmost significance for the student of Chapman who
must at all times interpret in terms both of the time and the man.

The character of Bussy illustrates the point; any understanding of him must of necessity be founded on the psychology and ethics which he seems to represent. And the ethical significance of Bussy's life as Chapman has depicted it is closely associated with the many-faceted psychology of which it is an expression.

Professor Parrot has stated that Bussy "is the embodiment of an idea which Chapman derived from the Stoics, that of the self-sufficiency, the all-sufficiency, of the virtuous man. Bussy, it is true, is far from virtuous in our modern sense of the word, but he is the very incarnation of *virtus* as the Romans understood it, 'the sum of all the bodily and mental excellences of man.' "[53] Viewed, however, from the vantage point of the sixteenth and early seventeenth centuries as well as from that of our own, this judgment seems not wholly accurate, for there is a difference between Bussy as "the very incarnation of [Roman] *virtus*" and a character "far from virtuous in our modern sense of the word." The Renaissance understanding of Stoic concepts should not be distorted by the introduction of criticism of a more modern cast, implying a distinction between *virtus* and "virtue" which to the man of the Renaissance had probably ceased to exist. We know that Elizabethan translations provided a clear picture of the ideal Stoical man. As we have already indicated in the Prologue to this study, that man was a virtuous individual of "self-sufficiency," even of "all-sufficiency"; likewise, he was the embodiment of the "mental excellences of man"; but he was also a man who refused to permit emotion, one of the so-called externals, to control his conduct. And Bussy does make his conduct subservient to his emotional impulses. His actions are all forged on the anvil of emotion, and he proceeds with the daring impetuosity of the sparks which fly from that anvil. He rarely gives the impression of a man whose sufficiency has been dictated by Reason rather than by passion—unlike a true Stoic, he moves from one thing to another without a goal. His desire for Tamyra, truly but an incident in his life, remains to a great degree the motivating force of the tragedy, and he is altogether willing to let himself, whom he considers virtuous, be carried along by the chance of Fortune to the point where Destiny refuses to be cheated. Bussy's tragic flaw, then, seems to result, not as Perkinson suggests from the fact that "Chapman . . . lays the tragic blame on Nature; or rather, he uses Bussy's fall as proof of her irrational ways,"[54] but rather from the fact that, according to Spencer, "The tragedy of Bussy is just this; he is swayed by desires over which he has no control."[55] The distinction is between an irrational Nature that Bussy could never control and an emotional inclination to action which lies within the possibility of a control he does not choose to exercise. In the light of Chapman's mental leanings toward Stoicism, the evidence seems to indicate, not that "Bussy . . . was a man after Chapman's own soul,"[56] but that he represented to Chapman the tragedy of the man without "doubts and scruples"[57] who decides "against the ethics of reasonable domination,"[58] thereby falling heir to a downfall of his own making. Stoicism did make a place for the man of action, yes, but it insisted that a life of action be consistent with a life based on Reason, completely divorced from the erratic dictates of emotion. Bussy's tragic flaw is that though he seems to be a complete man, his life lacks the control which Reason only can give: he must be added to the large collection of Renaissance slaves of passion.

Chapman's concern in his first tragedy with these characteristic elements of a Renaissance tragedy indicates he had not as yet developed a familiarity with many of those Stoic concepts that were to become the mental backdrops for his later literary endeavors. But if Chapman had not as yet come under the influence of those concepts that comprise the specific and more serious level of the ethics of Stoicism, an analysis of *Bussy* reveals that he had nevertheless become fully aware of several Stoic ideas that constitute the general and more popular patterns of the philosophy. Without changing the essential character of the tragedy, these ideas helped to direct its course.

We have suggested that this play opens and closes on two different themes. The first makes its appearance in the opening line of the first scene of Act I when Bussy is discovered on the stage soliloquizing about the state of the world and his own position in it—"Fortune, not reason, rules the state of things." Bussy's dictum is important in that it seems to establish the *milieu* in which the dramatic action is to unfold. Bussy goes on to ponder a world in which all things go contrary to the natural order, one in which

>   only Need
> Gives form and worth to every human seed,[59]

a world in which men are

>   merely great
> In their affected gravity of voice,
> Sourness of countenance, manners' cruelty,
> Authority, wealth, and all the spawn of Fortune.[60]

As Bussy views this scene, he sees that

> Man is a torch borne in the wind; a dream
> But of a shadow, summ'd with all his substance:[61]

and he concludes that when man's existence is completely dominated by Fortune, he must necessarily adopt some principle to give his life meaning:

> So when we wander furthest through the waves
> Of glassy Glory, and the gulfs of State,
> Topt with all titles, spreading all our reaches,
> As if each private arm would sphere the earth,
> We must to Virtue for her guide resort,
> Or we shall shipwrack in our safest port.[62]

The last two lines of this selection, the essence of much of Stoic doctrine, are particularly important coming from Bussy, for, though they announce the philosophy by which Bussy hopes to save himself in a world directed by the vagaries of Fortune as opposed to the concept of Destiny or Fate, the play is one in which both men and women refuse to be guided by the doctrine of virtue. We can only infer from Bussy's lines that the man who fails to pursue virtue for virtue's sake may achieve success by accepting Fortune's favors; certainly Bussy at first appears under her flag in this earliest of Chapman's tragedies.

Nor is Bussy the only character who emphasizes the importance of Fortune for those who become impatient with advancement. Having approached Bussy in his "green retreat," Monsieur almost at once presents the allurements of Fortune to draw Bussy to a life at Court:

> Do thou but bring
> Light to the banquet Fortune sets before thee.[63]

When Bussy expresses his contempt for the "well-head" of court life, Monsieur continues to urge him by recalling,

> The old Scythians
> Painted blind Fortune's powerful hands with wings
> To show her gifts come swift and suddenly,
> Which if her favourite be not swift to take,
> He loses them for ever.[64]

Won over, Bussy rationalizes his submission to Fortune when Monsieur has departed,

> If I may bring up a new fashion,
> And rise in Court for virtue, speed his plow![65]

But he also honestly admits to himself in conclusion,

> So no man riseth by his real merit,
> But when it cries clink in his raiser's spirit.
> Many will say, that cannot rise at all,
> Man's first hour's rise is first step to his fall.

I'll venture that; men that fall low must die,
As well as men cast headlong from the sky.[66]

The last two lines suggest clearly both the classical and medieval concept of Fortune's Wheel, a concept that Tamyra also recalls while she waits for the Friar to bring Bussy to her for the first time:

Make the violent wheels
Of Time and Fortune stand.[67]

Almost ironically, however, as if to deny Tamyra's plea for this stay of Time and Fortune's wheels, her husband, Montsurry, describes the success of Bussy's conquest of his wife in his characterization of the "great D'Ambois" as "Fortune's proud mushroom shot up in a night."[68]

Thus far in the play, Chapman has given little indication of the extent to which Fortune is to be permitted to control its tragic end. But in the second scene of Act III, in which the Guise and Bussy voice their differences before King Henry, the King sides with the latter, saying,

Nor had the full impartial hand of Nature
That all things gave in her original,
Without these definite terms of Mine and Thine,
Been turn'd unjustly to the hand of Fortune,
Had all preserv'd her in her prime, like D'Ambois.[69]

The lines have interesting implications, for Chapman's audience knew then, as the modern reader also knows, that Henry's words are specious; Bussy has thus far proved himself to be the archexample of the man who has entrusted his rise not to "the full impartial hand of Nature" but to "the hand of Fortune." If Chapman had then permitted Bussy's downfall to spring from a seeming dedication of his life to the principles of merit and impartial Nature, when in reality his rise had sprung from the notion that "the bold are Fortune's darlings,"[70] the tragedy of Bussy would have seemed to present the catastrophe as a Nemesis for overweening pride. For Bussy's actions had not been controlled by a sense of justice, but dictated by his desire for realization of a personality which made its own laws.

Bussy continues in his exalted, insolent manner for another act, however, before Chapman actually shifts his attention from Fortune and turns to the opposite concept of Fate or Destiny as the explanation of Bussy's downfall. Although Tamyra in Scene 1 of Act III does justify her yielding to Bussy by turning to Destiny for an excuse:

> It is not I, but urgent destiny,
> That (as great statesmen for their general end
> In politic justice, make poor men offend)
> Enforceth my offence to make it just.
> What shall weak dames do, when th' whole work of nature
> Hath a strong finger in each one of us?[71]

there is a difference between justifying a single act of human frailty by means of Destiny and depicting tragedy through the same medium, difference only of degree though it is.

Professor Parrott, also looking upon D'Ambois' lust for Tamyra as "plainly enough only an incident in Bussy's career,"[72] believes "that . . . the true theme of the tragedy of *Bussy D'Ambois*" is "the struggle of such a character with his environment, the combat of the individualist against the world, and his fall—not so much at the hands of Guise and Monsieur, as of Death and Destiny."[73] That Chapman, like the Stoics, conceived Death as the work of Destiny, a conception that enabled them to explain much of what happened to man in the world, is explicit in the final scenes of the play. After Bussy and Monsieur have insulted each other almost to the point of physical violence in his presence, Henry comments as he leads Bussy away:

Here's nought but whispering with us; like a calm
Before a tempest, when the silent air
Lays her soft ear close to the earth to hearken
For that she fears steals on to ravish her;
Some fate doth join our ears to hear it coming.
Come, my brave eagle, let's to covert fly;
I see Almighty Æther in the smoke
Of all his clouds descending, and the sky
Hid in the dim ostents of tragedy.[74]

The theme of Fate makes its next appearance in the form of the late
Friar who appears briefly to Bussy in the latter's house to forewarn
him of "bloody deeds past and to come," and departs on the ominous
note, "I cannot stay; a fate doth ravish me."[75] After the "Umbra
Friar" has gone, Bussy recalls the Spirits who had promised to return if he needed them. When he questions Behemoth,

                                        Who then
Will my dear mistress send?

Behemoth answers,

                              I must not tell thee.

Bus.   Who lets thee?
Beh.   Fate.
Bus.   Who are Fate's ministers?
Beh.   The Guise and Monsieur.
Bus.   A fit pair of shears
        To cut the threads of kings and kingly spirits,
        And consorts fit to sound forth harmony
        Set to the falls of kingdoms![76]

But Bussy refuses to stay in spite of Behemoth's warning, choosing
rather to follow Destiny:

I must fare well, however, though I die,
My death consenting with his augury:

> Should not my powers obey when she commands,
> My motion must be rebel to my will,
> My will to life.[77]

Even when Bussy learns that Monsieur and the Guise have ambushed him in Montsurry's house, he still refuses to believe that Fate will deliver him into the hands of the hired assassins:

> Fate is more strong than arms, and sly than treason,
> And I at all parts buckled in my fate.[78]

And when he is wounded by an exchange of pistol shots, he can only cry out,

> O, then the coward Fates
> Have maim'd themselves, and ever lost their honour,[79]

and ask the Umbra of the dead Friar in the face of the inevitable to excuse his enemies:

> Forbear them, father; 'tis enough for me
> That Guise and Monsieur, Death and Destiny,
> Come behind D'Ambois.[80]

Fate, however, though it brings Bussy to his death, fails to conquer his proud spirit:

> O, my heart is broken!
> Fate nor these murtherers, Monsieur nor the Guise,
> Have any glory in my death, but this,
> This killing spectacle, this prodigy;[81]

and he dies, breathing some of his former glory:

> O frail condition of strength, valour, virtue,
> In me (like warning fire upon the top
> Of some steep beacon, on a steeper hill)
> Made to express it: like a falling star
> Silently glanc'd, that like a thunderbolt
> Look'd to have stuck and shook the firmament.[82]

There can be little doubt that *Bussy D'Ambois* ends on the tragic note Chapman had determined upon, for at no time did he lose either the control or the direction of his material. It is impossible to determine whether or not it was Chapman's interest in Stoicism which made him consciously contrast Fortune and Destiny. But a study of the text does seem to indicate that Chapman ended with an interpretation of his material which the opening lines do not suggest, for the difference between events motivated by fickle Fortune and those necessitated by the dictates of unrelenting Destiny is as marked in the play as it is in Stoicism itself. On the one hand, we have the concept of action over which man has some control, for he need not choose to subject himself to the buffetings of chance; on the other, one of Fate over which man has no control and with whose decrees he must acquiesce. His rebellion, although it contains the idea of struggle inherent in all dramatic action, does not include any hope of salvation. If the Stoics, whose writings he knew so well, did not incline Chapman to distrust the whims of the Goddess Fortuna, medieval[83] as well as early Renaissance literature often provided examples of her instability. By way of contrast, the idea of Fate from which escape is almost nonexistent appears with relentless regularity on many of the pages of Homer's *Iliad* and *Odyssey*. Furthermore, this seeming predilection of Chapman for the essentially nondramatic concept of Fate indicates his early inclination toward ideas which did not often permit the struggle that is the essence of the theater.

This tragedy of *Bussy D'Ambois* is interesting also for other evidences of what may very well be called Chapman's thinking aloud, particularly about the theory of Nature. Monsieur's reference to Nature just before he tempts Bussy to give himself over to Fortune,

> There's but a thread betwixt me and a crown,
> I would not wish it cut, unless by nature,[84]

leads to the interpretation that Monsieur would not wish the thread between the Crown and himself cut unless this action represented the inevitable end that Nature had long since determined. Such a conclusion, of course, has inherent in it the idea of Destiny, and bears out Perkinson's contention that in *Bussy* "Nature is visualized as not only the creator of man, but also as the fashioner of his fate."[85] Bussy himself resumes the analysis of the meaning of Nature after Henry, at Monsieur's request, has excused his killing of Barrisor, L'Anou, and Pyrhot:

> This is a grace that (on my knees redoubled),
> I crave, to double this my short life's gift,
> And shall your royal bounty centuple,
> That I may so make good what God and Nature
> Have given me for my good.[86]

Here Chapman, like the Stoics, closely aligns God and Nature, making them the coauthors of man and also granting them the power of allotting to each individual the development of his own potential good. That Chapman conceived this development on a highly ethical plane where the individual remained the chief protagonist is revealed in the lines which continue those quoted above:

> since I am free,
> (Offending no just law), let no law make
> By any wrong it does, my life her slave:
> When I am wrong'd, and that law fails to right me,
> Let me be king myself (as man was made),
> And do a justice that exceeds the law;
> If my wrong pass the power of single valour
> To right and expiate; then be you my king,
> And do a right, exceeding law and nature:
> Who to himself is law, no law doth need,
> Offends no law, and is a king indeed.[87]

Such a statement of belief is challenging for several reasons:

Elizabethan drama, which so often reflects the problems of the period for the ruler and the ruled, is filled with many such allusions, and Chapman himself adopted this question as one of his motivating ideas, as we shall have frequent occasion to note; again, the concept that he who is a law unto himself, provided such law be rational, is above all other laws is one of the chief tenets of Stoicism. But Chapman's adherence to such a doctrine was here as elsewhere in his tragedies an enervating factor, for in porportion as man's pursuit of what God and Nature have in store for him is mere following of Destiny rather than struggling against it, it lacks dramatic vitality. We are, therefore, left to watch a dramatic essay written in heroic vein, not a dramatic action suited to stage production.

That Monsieur and the Guise renew the discussion of nature in the second scene of Act V is significant because their words follow immediately Tamyra's forced admission of her guilt with Bussy to her husband, Montsurry, and foreshadow the collapse of both their fortunes. Monsieur remarks,

> Now shall we see that Nature hath no end
> In her great works responsive to their worths;
> That she, that makes so many eyes and souls
> To see and foresee, is stark blind herself . . .
>   so Nature lays
> A deal of stuff together, and by use,
> Or by the mere necessity of matter,
> Ends such a work, fills it, or leaves it empty
> Of strength or virtue, error or clear truth,
> Not knowing what she does; but usually
> Gives that which we call merit to a man,
> And believe should arrive him on huge riches,
> Honour, and happiness, that effects his ruin.[88]

Monsieur begins with a denial that Nature can create a good end, a denial which Bussy had earlier advanced to King Henry. Now we are told that perhaps because she has to "foresee" for so many, Nature is herself "blind," "hath no end," and does not know "what she does"; in fact, Monsieur's conclusions that Nature heaps merit, honor, and happiness on a man only to effect his ruin is no true delineation of Nature at all, but one much more descriptive of a fanciful and errant Fortune. The Guise, however, does not accept Monsieur's exposition, and following the allusion that Nature may ruin a man whom she has already advanced, he counters with a critical evaluation of Monsieur both as a man and a kingly aspirant:

> He that observes but like a worldly man
> That which doth oft succeed and by th' events
> Values the worth of things, will think it true
> That Nature works at random, just with you:
> But with as much proportion she may make
> A thing that from the feet up to the throat
> Hath all the wondrous fabric man should have,
> And leave it headless, for a perfect man,
> As give a full man valour, virtue, learning,
> Without an end more excellent than those
> On whom she no such worthy part bestows.[89]

Although the phrase "a worldly man" is here not directed only to Monsieur, yet it is Monsieur who has acted as the worldly man in his attempts to achieve the crown—by trying to use Bussy for his own worldly gain almost to the "killing of the King." And the Guise's reference to a seemingly mutable Nature is a clear-cut characterization of Monsieur's influence at Court, favoring Bussy's almost meteoric rise, an advancement which miscarried because Bussy proved more eager to satisfy his own passion for Tamyra than to help Monsieur become king. It is the Guise's suggestion, then, that Monsieur and Bussy as well are the guilty ones; it is they, not Nature, who have worked "at random." Furthermore, he goes on to point out that Nature may make a "headless" man who is perfect from "the feet up to the throat"; yet even a man of "valour, virtue, learning" is no more worthy than he who has been endowed with none of these attributes unless he has an "excellent end" in mind. But can either Monsieur or Bussy truly qualify as men of valor, virtue, learning? Can the "end" which they desire be said to be "excellent" in any sense of the word? Since the answer to both questions must be in the negative, the Guise's whole speech must be regarded as a refutation of Monsieur's thinking.

Monsieur, however, either does not follow the Guise's implications or he refuses to yield the point, for he answers,

> Yet shall you see it here: here will be one
> Young, learned, valiant, virtuous, and full mann'd;
> One on whom Nature spent so rich a hand
> That with an ominous eye she wept to see
> So much consum'd her virtuous treasury.[90]

We must accept Monsieur's characterization of Bussy without being altogether able to admit its accuracy, for, typical Renaissance hero though he may be, Bussy does not appear in action as that perfect or complete man, at all times learned, virtuous, and full-mann'd, one whom a decaying Nature seeks haphazardly to destroy with an unwarranted fate. The argument as developed by Chapman becomes largely a matter of philosophical exposition, dictated by the demands of dramatic necessity—an attempt at a reasoned solution of some sort for Bussy's eventual fall—approaching the familiar concept of Fortune:

> So this whole man
> (That will not wind with every crooked way,

Trod by the servile world) shall reel and fall
Before the frantic puffs of blind-born chance,[91]

for it is Fortune rather than any theory of Nature as Monsieur tries
to fashion it that is inevitably suggested by "blind-born chance."
Then, too, Monsieur himself reverts to Fortune for a comparison
with which to conclude his thinking upon the subject:

Not so the sea raves on the Lybian sands,
Tumbling her billows in each others' neck;
Not so the surges of the Euxine sea
(Near to the frosty pole, where free Boötes
From those dark deep waves turns his radiant team)
Swell, being enrag'd, even from their inmost drop,
As Fortune swings about the restless state
Of virtue, now thrown into all men's hate.[92]

If, then, we were faced with only Monsieur's views expressed in
this short scene, we should have to accept fully Perkinson's statement, "But to account for the super-man's vulnerability, Chapman
presents a curious theory of Nature on whom the blame is thrown.
. . . Chapman . . . lays the tragic blame on Nature; or rather, he
uses Bussy's fall as proof of her irrational ways."[93] But we are faced
with a speech of the Guise's, too, which we feel prevents to a great
extent Monsieur's comments from being accepted without qualification. For the idea of a "full man" lacking a worthwhile end
coupled with Monsieur's own reversion to the concept of Fortune,
almost synonymous with his utterances about Nature, would seem
to indicate that we should not push his remarks on Nature to the
point where they must assume a greater importance in an interpretation of Chapman than is inherent in them.

Perkinson also comments in his highly provocative article, "It
would seem probable, then, that Chapman's theory of Nature in
Bussy is not immediately or primarily philosophic, in the way his

ideas have been regarded, but dramatically utilitarian."[94] Here
Perkinson's comment seems essentially correct. And weight is
added to his conclusion when we consider that a concept of a decaying Nature is also foreign to Chapman's mind, which often
recognizes a world that is out of joint, but which rarely succumbs
to a theory of general social disruption, so closely related to the
"decay of Nature" theme. Like the Stoics whom he was later to
emulate in his tragic heroes to an ever increasing extent, he, too,
sought always to find a means of finding security, no matter the
condition of the world at large. The concept of Nature to which
he seems to have clung at all times was not widely separated from
that of Destiny and God's will, a premeditated and active force in
man's life which Chapman's classical studies again and again demonstrated could not be avoided.

The importance of *Bussy D'Ambois* as Chapman's first experiment with dramatic tragedy lies in its trial-and-error techniques.
Since Chapman tests a number of ideas as he writes, it is difficult to
weigh its value and its purpose as an exposition of any single idea
or form. Given over as it is to a consideration of psychological and
philosophical concepts of a highly ethical temper, it moves from
the idea of tragedy as the expression of Fortune's whims to that of
the forces of Destiny which must have their way; it stops to consider the effects of a God and Nature, both irrational, upon man's
life, but concludes that man himself and not Nature is responsible
for his own downfall; it explores the fate of a man and a woman,
one of whom refuses to follow the path of Reason, while the other
realizes clearly the tragedy that must follow a choice of unbridled
passion but is powerless to act reasonably; it uses the old theme of
revenge for honor, including the device of the rack; it employs the
world of the supernatural with its ghosts and spirits; and it calls
upon the abused servant for comic relief. It would not have been
surprising if Chapman had failed to achieve unity among such a

welter of confusing and sometimes confused detail; but the very variety of elements seems to establish unity, "a unity which," as Smith writes, "seems to preclude all division into parts,"[95] and the drama emerges "in the matter of construction," at least, "Chapman's masterpiece in tragedy."[96] The success that *Bussy* enjoyed on the stage emphasizes the fact that Chapman could on occasion rise to the demands of his art.

Though the patter of Stoicism current in the early seventeenth century must be considered in any analysis of the tragedy, it does not as yet seriously affect either Chapman's thinking or his skill in stagecraft; the ethics of Stoicism do not intrude as a consistent force either upon the dramatist's development of character or upon his handling of plot. That both Tamyra and Bussy reflect, however, Chapman's awareness of the fundamentals of Stoic thought is certainly evident. It is equally obvious that Bussy's reaction to approaching death is too much like that of Byron, Clermont, and Cato to be mere coincidence. Yet Bussy's final attitude does not rob his death of tragic significance since his fall can in no sense be compared with that of a defeatist. He remains glorious in death despite the fact that the tragedy has been of his own making, for he has been willing to engage in irrational conflict with the world, believing that he would succeed where others had failed. His devotion to the Marlovian ideal of the superman remains in part at least the measure of his heroic stature. To this extent, Chapman still remains impervious to the influence of the Stoic ethics; to this extent, Chapman's artistry remains unaffected by contempt for the emotions and Stoic insistence that man live according to rational principles of virtuous conduct. This independence of even the conventions of Stoicism accounts in no small way for the singular success of *Bussy D'Ambois,* a success that Chapman was never again to achieve.

But *Bussy* is interesting for other reasons. We see in this tragedy that Chapman was looking forward to the writing of another tragedy, as the *Epilogue* of the revision of 1610 reveals. It seems likely that as Chapman's study of the hero gained scope through his translations of *The Iliad* and *The Odyssey* made at the time of the writing of *Bussy*, he saw an opportunity for a sequel in which the man of action so dominated by passion could be unfavourably compared, in his mind at least, with a protagonist who lived according to a totally different concept—that of quiet reflection typified by the Stoic insistence upon the calm and tranquil mind from which emotion had been deliberately excluded. If such was the case, then Bussy must be regarded as a kind of foil to a man such as Clermont. And it must be regarded as equally significant that save for the *Byron* plays which fall in time between *Bussy* and *The Revenge of Bussy*, the pattern achieved in the latter play remained very much the same for *The Tragedy of Caesar and Pompey* and *The Tragedy of Chabot Admiral of France*. When we remember that it was in 1611-12 that Chapman found in Epictetus the focus of his interest in the Stoical man, *Bussy D'Ambois* becomes doubly interesting. For it is the precursor of Chapman's preoccupation with Stoicism as a way of life, as a protection against his own world, in which examples of the Renaissance hero were never lacking. Bussy was cast in the mold of the hero whose personal tragedy fills many a page of the history of the period. With the exception of Byron, Chapman had finished with the Bussylike individualist who brings moral chaos to the world by his selfish and antisocial ways as a man of *virtus*. In *The Revenge of Bussy* he turns to a consideration of another individualist, foreign to Renaissance ideology, the man who, quietly pursuing his destiny with integrity, does not affect the world except as he deliberately removes himself from it. Chapman's first tragedy then becomes important because it indicates that Stoical ideas were beginning to direct his thinking, though, fortunately for his later reputation, they had not yet affected his art.

CHAPTER TWO: THE CONSPIRACY AND TRAGEDY OF CHARLES DUKE OF BYRON

> His country's love
> He yet thirsts, *not the fair shades of himself;*
> Of which empoison'd spring when Policy drinks,
> He bursts in growing great, and rising, sinks:
> Which now behold in our conspirator,
> And see in his revolt how honour's flood
> Ebbs into air, *when men are great, not good.*
>
> Prologus, *Byron's Conspiracy,*
> 11. 18-24 (italics mine).

SOME THREE or four years after *Bussy D'Ambois* and two or three before *The Revenge of Bussy D'Ambois,* late in 1607 or early in 1608,[1] Chapman wrote *The Conspiracy* and *The Tragedy of Charles Duke of Byron,* two plays that appear much more unified than the earlier *Bussy* tragedy. Since the title page of the first edition (1608) states that they were "acted lately in two playes, at the Black-Friers,"[2] it would be interesting to know what arrangements then obtained for their presentation, particularly when the second is so necessary to the first. The close tie between the two *Byron* dramas would seem to have required one continuous performance.

THE CONSPIRACY

If we may call Bussy a man of action, we may also say that Byron represents a continuation of this character pattern—they are both men who by disposition always aspire to what is above and beyond them. Byron, in particular, is not satisfied, soldier that he is, to rest on his laurels in headquarters. He must be dashing off to the outposts of empire about his king's business—and his own as well; he is as much at home in Elizabeth's court or at Brussels as on the battlefield from which he has sprung. His horizons are not of the mind, but of the places in which he demands respect as the King's distinguished servant. It is not enough, however, that he should have risen so high; he, too, like Monsieur in *Bussy D'Ambois,* would even be King. *Byron's Conspiracy,* then, develops in large measure in the world of individual ambition outlined in Chapman's first tragedy, and we shall find that Byron himself is no more of a Stoical man than Bussy.

The last lines of the "Prologus" contain the implication that this play is also to be one of Fortune's making; Fortune's Wheel is suggested by the line "He bursts in growing great, and, rising, sinks." When Roiseau reports to King Henry the way in which Byron was "courted" in Brussels, the King finds the explanation of Byron's behavior in his instability:

> It may be he dissembled, or suppose
> He be a little tainted, men whom virtue
> Forms with the stuff of Fortune, great and gracious,
> Must needs partake with Fortune in her humour
> Of instability, and are like to shafts
> Grown crook'd with standing, which to rectify
> Must twice as much be bow'd another way.[3]

Later, Savoy praises Byron to the King, that he may widen the gap already existing between him and Byron. The King at first agrees with Savoy's compliments,

> No question he sets valour in his height.
> And hath done service to an equal pitch,
> Fortune attending him with fit events,
> To all his vent'rous and well-laid attempts.[4]

To which Savoy adds,

> Fortune to him was Juno to Alcides . . .
> Fortune is so far from his creditress
> That she owes him much, for in him her looks
> Are lovely, modest, and magnanimous,
> Constant, victorious.[5]

Byron himself goes to La Brosse, the Astrologer, presenting his disguised person as one whom Fortune controls:

>   daily and hourly proof
> Tells us prosperity is at highest degree
> The fount and handle of calamity:
> Like dust before a whirlwind those men fly
> That prostrate on the grounds of Fortune lie;
> And being great, like trees that broadest sprout,
> Their own top-heavy state grubs up their root.[6]

Just as in *Bussy,* however, Chapman again implies a criticism of the concept of Fortune as an adequate explanation of man's fall. The first scene of Act IV, as we now have it, purports to be a verbal account of Byron's interview with Elizabeth at the English court, where, as Byron is about to depart, a Councillor tells him,

> He that wins empire with the loss of faith
> Out-buys it, and will bankrout; you have laid
> A brave foundation by the hand of virtue;
> Put not the roof to fortune: foolish statuaries,
> That under little saints suppose great bases
> Make less to sense the saints; and so, where Fortune
> Advanceth vile minds to states great and noble,
> She much the more exposeth them to shame,
> Not able to make good and fill their bases
> With a conformed structure.[7]

There can be little doubt in the light of this evidence that Chapman at least wishes to suggest as the cause of Byron's eventual fall his too great reliance on Fortune's favors. In *Bussy D'Ambois* the theory of a Fortune tragedy is simply stated as a *raison d'etre* of the tragedy itself; in *The Conspiracy,* however, though Chapman uses the Fortune theme as an explanation of the tragedy that ensues, he has now become critical of it. It is no longer merely a question of stating the theory, for the playwright has found that Fortune, as conceived in the above selection, is

> Not able to make good and fill their bases
> With a conformed structure.

There is no indication as *The Conspiracy* closes of what Chapman will choose as a substitute for his reliance on Fortune as the wellspring of the tragedy, but it is interesting to note that at the end of his second tragedy, he has twice rejected Fortune as a satisfactory agent for the development of tragedy.

Interesting, too, is the fact that the Nature theme is barely glanced at in *The Conspiracy.* Picoté briefly recalls to the reader the discussion in *Bussy* between Monsieur and the Guise in his attempt to encourage Byron to follow his ambition:

> The habit of a servile loyalty
> Is reckon'd now amongst privations,
> With blindness, dumbness, deafness, silence, death;
> All which are neither natures by themselves
> Nor substances, but mere decays of form,
> And absolute decessions of nature.[8]

In this passage Nature holds no high place, having again become mutable and undependable. Chapman, however, differentiates between affairs at the French court and the English court, where by contrast he indicates

there's a queen
Where Nature keeps her state, and State her Court,
Wisdom her study, Continence her fort.[9]

Byron himself is reported to have told Elizabeth:

"So in your government, conclusive Nature
(Willing to end her excellence in earth
When your foot shall be set upon the stars)
Shows all her sovereign beauties, ornaments,
Virtues and raptures; overtakes her works
In former empires, makes them but your foils;
Swells to her full sea, and again doth drown
The world in admiration of your crown."[10]

Aside, then, from the comparison that sets the English form of
government above the French but does not affect the course of dramatic action, the major reference to Nature in *The Conspiracy* indicates that Byron, like Monsieur, is to pay scant respect to Nature's
laws, taking as his excuse that in a topsy-turvy world, her true
worth has been rightfully impugned and nothing is to be gained by
following her.

Similarly, the revenge motif does not motivate the action of *The
Conspiracy* to the same extent as in *Bussy*. La Fin fancies himself
wronged because the King frowns upon him as "the centre to im-
piety,"[11] and comments to Byron,

Since the King hath wrong'd me
He thinks I'll hurt myself; no, no, my lord,
I know that all the kings in Christendom,
If they should join in my revenge, would prove
Weak foes to him, still having you to friend.[12]

And when King Henry openly laughs at Byron's boastful recital of
his own past glories, Byron, much in the manner of the Nuntius in
Bussy, calls out,

Respect, Revenge; Slaughter, repay for laughter. . . .
Forth, Vengeance, then, and open wounds in him
Shall let in Spain and Savoy.[13]

D'Auvergne does not adhere to this course of action, and restrains Byron, who for a second time offers to draw his sword against his king:

O my lord,
This is too large a license given your fury;
Give time to it; what reason suddenly
Cannot extend, respite doth oft supply.[14]

But Byron will not be soothed; he replies,

While respite holds revenge the wrong redoubles,
And so the shame of sufferance.[15]

With these rather inconclusive references to revenge in the final scene of the last act, the subject is dropped as Byron kneels before the King, yielding to Henry's plea that he give up his "disease." The audience is then dismissed with an amazing conclusion to the same scene that acts as a kind of interlude between *The Conspiracy* and *The Tragedy* which follows closely.

Like *Bussy,* then, *The Conspiracy* is not primarily interesting for its various allusions to already familiar themes. The play achieves its importance in the character of Byron, and, to a lesser degree, in the characters of King Henry and La Fin. From the opening lines of the play forward, too, echoes of Bussy surround Byron, showing in marked degree that when Chapman came to the writing of *The Conspiracy,* he was creating a man like Bussy, one whose life represented the same dissatisfaction with the differences between his present state and that for which he felt his worth qualified him. Roncas pictures Byron as

a man
Of matchless valour . . . ever happy
In all encounters, which were still made good
With an unwearied sense of any toil,
Having continued fourteen days together
Upon his horse; his blood is not voluptuous,
Nor much inclined to women; his desires
Are higher than his state, and his deserts
Not much short of the most he can desire.[16]

Thus far the report of Byron stamps him as the kind of man in whom Chapman was for the time being deeply interested. In keeping with the fact that Byron is "not much inclined to women," the Dramatis Personae includes only *"Three* Ladies *at the French Court,"* and, while women do appear with speaking roles in the remaining tragedies, no one of them approaches Tamyra's pivotal position in *Bussy.* Byron's "matchless valour," his boundless energy, and his praiseworthy "deserts" also go far to recommend him as Chapman's own, at least in so far as his emotional appeal is concerned, even though Chapman's reasonable mind was finally to reject him. True to the nature of the tragic hero, however, Byron has a weakness that is predestined to prove fatal:

Ambition also cheek by cheek doth march
With that excess of glory, both sustain'd
With an unlimited fancy that the King,
Nor France itself, without him can subsist.[17]

After this detail has been added to the portrait, even Savoy's answer, "He is the man, my lord, I come to win,"[18] is unnecessary to the early conclusion that, in spite of any sympathetic inclination Chapman may have for Byron, he is nonetheless doomed, for the conventions of Stoicism denied a place to the man who persisted in being violently discontented with his lot. Later, Chapman was to read in Epictetus' *Discourses* a reaffirmation of this belief: "When a man has his proper station in life, he does not hanker after what is beyond him."[19] And nowhere in Chapman does one find any justification for the overthrow of virtuous authority. Byron, therefore, begins to emerge as one who hankers "after what is beyond him," even though his King has raised him because of his worth to his "proper station." Disruption of this relationship meant disruption of the social order; indirectly, then, Byron's "unlimited fancy" has foreshadowed his downfall before he has once appeared on the stage, for the Jacobean audience knew even better than we the problems that such a situation posed, and there dared be no doubt of the outcome.

Even before La Fin appears, he is described as one who will fit the plans for Byron's future:

> There is another discontented spirit
> Now here in Court.[20]

Bussylike, La Fin tells Henry,

> I must confess my fortunes are declin'd
> But neither my deservings nor my mind . . .
> man's right to everything
> Wanes with his wealth, wealth is his surest king;
> Yet Justice should be still indifferent.
> The overplus of kings, in all their might,
> *Is but to piece out the defects of right.*[21]

And while Henry's criticism of La Fin makes him more of a piece with the wily Monsieur than Bussy—

> Thou . . .
> Hast no heart but to hurt, and eat'st thy heart,
> If it but think of doing any good:
> Thou . . .
> Cozen'st with virtue—[22]

La Fin stands as a ready companion for Byron, who says he will

> dissolve in changing; 'tis so full
> Of pleasure not to be contain'd in flesh:
> To fear a violent good abuseth goodness,
> 'Tis immortality to die aspiring,
> As if a man were taken quick to heaven . . .
>   To have stuff and form,
> And to lie idle, fearful, and unus'd,
> Nor form nor stuff shows.[23]

Brulart's almost Stoic utterance to D'Aumale in another connection is a fitting commentary on the kind of life La Fin and Byron have thus far advocated:

>   That which men enforce
> By their own wilfulness, they must endure
> With willing patience and without complaint.[24]

Chapman has portrayed Byron as a more rational protagonist than Bussy, who is incapable of making a choice that will give a meaningful direction to his life. Byron is fashioned from sterner stuff; his decision to better his station is no blind following of ambitious aspiration. And because Byron believes he is acting according to Reason, he appears even in *The Conspiracy* as a man whose goal represents a unity of purpose that Bussy never achieved. Byron could never have understood Bussy's impulsive actions, for the former's creed,

> I have a will and faculties of choice,
> To do, or not to do: and reason why
> I do, or not do this:[25]

is the antithesis of Bussy's every move. It is a mark of Chapman's artistic development that Byron's character emerges whole from actions he himself has planned and decided upon, regardless of any judgment placed upon unbounded ambition.

The basic character of Bussy and Byron, both of whom have a remarkable faculty for making long speeches either in explanation or in lieu of their actions, is clearly demonstrated in the often quoted lines which follow. Fundamentally, down to the very last line, they belong as much to Bussy as to Byron, whose lines they are. Free, adventurous, full of the zest for living, they seem to typify the Bussylike man whom Chapman so patently admires in the character of Byron, even if he was to conclude in *The Tragedy of Byron* that the world was not yet ripe for liberties within the social order such as those Byron urges:

> be free, all worthy spirits,
> And stretch yourselves for greatness and for height,
> Untruss your slaveries; you have height enough
> Beneath this steep heaven to use all your reaches;
> 'Tis too far off to let you, or respect you.
> Give me a spirit that on this life's rough sea
> Loves t'have his sails fill'd with a lusty wind,
> Even till his sail-yards tremble, his masts crack,
> And his rapt ship run on her side so low
> That she drinks water, and her keel plows air.
> There is no danger to a man that knows
> What life and death is; there's not any law
> Exceeds his knowledge; neither is it lawful
> That he should stoop to any other law.
> He goes before them, and commands them all,
> *That to himself is a law rational.*[26]

Not characteristic of Bussy, however, is Byron's insistence in the last line upon man's rational behavior. Bussy, too, had emphasized the individuality of the man who insisted that he was his own law, but the qualification of that law's being rational seems never to have occurred to him.

Yet Byron's recognition of the importance of man's governing his actions by rational law applies only in theory, for, when he becomes a suitor to his King for "the citadel of Bourg," Henry denies his request with this explanation:

> I am enforc'd:
> I have no power, more than yourself, in things
> That are beyond my reason.[27]

If Byron were consistent, he would then be content. That he is not adds that element of suspense which springs from the struggle of the individual against a world he seeks to change. He rants and vows, like Bussy, to be his "own king." But Chapman says in effect that no man can so distort the social structure, for, despite Byron's expressed desire to avenge his slight, he finally bows to the King's warning:

> And therefore leave them and be true to me,
> Or you'll be left by all; or be like one
> That in cold nights will needs have all the fire,
> And there is held by others, and embrac'd
> Only to burn him; your fire will be inward,
> Which not another deluge can put out.[28]

Byron falls to his knees before his King to acknowledge his "madness" and to "rise by absolute merit," forgiven.

Since the play ends shortly after this point with a sprightly encounter between the ladies and gentlemen of the Court, we realize that the five acts of *The Conspiracy* do not constitute a play, much less a tragedy. They gain meaning only when they become an integral part of the further action Chapman continued from his source[29] in *The Tragedy of Charles Duke of Byron.*

THE TRAGEDY

The first line of this sequel to *The Conspiracy* indicates at once that the fault in Byron did not die with his forgiveness, for Henry expresses surprise at "Byron fall'n in so trait'rous a relapse."[30] And Janin reminds us once more of Byron's tragic flaw, "The fatal thirst of his ambition."[31] Henry's reaction to Byron's "relapse" marks him as a character to be reckoned with in any attempt to portray the development of Chapman's mind, for his concern with Byron reveals certain ideas which are more clearly Stoical than any thus far encountered. In the first place, the King does not understand Byron's sacrificing his integrity:

But far it flies my thoughts that such a spirit,
So active, valiant, and vigilant,
Can see itself transform'd with such wild furies.[32]

The King thinks he may find the explanation in the character of La Fin,

since his state,
Grown to decay and he to discontent,
Comes near the ambitious plight of Duke Byron.[33]

Byron himself in *The Conspiracy* had come to the same conclusion:

He has a will to me, and dares not show it;
His state decay'd, and he disgrac'd, distracts him.[34]

The remainder of the action from this point in Act I forward is nothing more than a denouement based on Henry's analysis of the renewal of Byron's conspiracy and his determination not to see "A trait'rous subject foil me."[35]

It should be noted in passing that as early as Scene I of Act I Chapman tells us that he is finished with the Fortune-tragedy—Fortune will not suffice to explain the downfall of the man who would overthrow the natural order. When the young Dauphin is brought to him, Henry prays,

> Let him by virtue quite [cut] off from Fortune
> Her feather'd shoulders and her winged shoes,
> And thrust from her light feet her turning stone
> That she may never tarry by his throne.[36]

The remaining four acts of *The Tragedy* are chiefly interesting for their insistence upon two themes, one of which—the proper relation between subject and king—constitutes the major part of the story of Byron's fall; the other of which—the triumph of justice over mercy—shows Chapman reverting to an early English conception of tragedy in which the demands of justice are for a time held in abeyance while the possibilities of an appeal to mercy are considered.

The two opposed points of view regarding the relation of the ruler and the ruled are represented by Henry and Byron, respectively, comprising for the most part the matter of Scene 3 of Act I through Scene 2 of Act IV. On the one hand, King Henry stands for the tradition of sovereign right which cannot tolerate traitorous subjects, since the subject owes the same allegiance to his King as the King in turn owes to his God.[37] Stoic doctrine fully approves Henry's self-adopted position as God's earthly representative. Since the Stoics believed that Nature truly reflects the will of God, it followed that subjects must respect and obey the ruler who honestly tries to prevent Nature's law from being inverted. Byron's "unnatural conspiracy"[38] therefore leaves Henry no alternative but to make him, if he will not submit to authority, the "first example of" his "forced justice." Since Byron remains to his King that "unthankful man," and will not acknowledge his error, Henry is forced to decide,

> The decent ceremonies of my laws
> And their solemnities shall be observed
> With all their sternness and severity.[39]

If justice is to be maintained, the ruled must submit to the will of
the ruler:

> But you disdain submission, not rememb'ring,
> That (in intents urg'd for the common good)
> He that shall hold his peace, being charg'd to speak,
> Doth all the peace and nerves of empire break;
> Which on your [Byron's] conscience lie.[40]

On the other hand, Byron represents the independence of the
subject who cannot tolerate servility since the ruler owes an allegiance, too, no less important than that owed him. Byron gives the
topic a cynical flavor when he insists in an injured manner,

> we must not be more true to kings
> Than kings are to their subjects.[41]

Nor does he draw upon our sympathy by arguing that God

> (knows kings are not made by art,
> But right of Nature, nor by treachery propp'd,
> But simple virtue),[42]

for the logic of his argument is nullified by our realization that he
himself is not acting from the causes of "simple virtue." He must
finally appear as much condemned by his own words:

> Where I, in those assumptions, may scorn
> And speak contemptuously of all the world,
> For any equal yet I ever found;[43]

as by Janin's:

> A subject's confidence in any merit
> Against his Sovereign, that makes him presume
> To fly too high, approves him like a cloud
> That makes a show as it did hawk at kingdoms.[44]

Nor does Byron's contention that "he can no way worthily maintain/ His prince's honour that neglects his own"[45] in any way justify the subject who defies his king for the purpose of selfish gain.

Any understanding of the stand Byron chooses to defend must come through the realization that he is above all a soldier[46] who knows and loves the field of battle as only he who has never been vanquished can enjoy it, as a place where valor, strength, and victory are the marks of success. Henry himself early in *The Conspiracy* recognizes in La Fin, Byron's accomplice for a time, the man to whom war is life itself—"Thou art at peace with nothing but with war",[47] and Byron's contempt for "the most base fruits of a settled peace!"[48] is but the contrary of Henry's judgments upon La Fin; Byron does not comprehend man's tilling the "dirty fields" in an attempt to

> make them better than when cruel war
> Frighted from thence the sweaty labourer;
> But men themselves, instead of bearing fruits,
> Grow rude and foggy, overgrown with weeds,
> Their spirits and freedoms smother'd in their ease.[49]

By his own words Byron stands comparable to the Earl of Essex—

> The matchless Earl of Essex, whom some make
> (In their most sure divinings of my death)
> A parallel with me in life and fortune—[50]

and for that very reason he must fall; as Janin points out to Henry,

> Princes, you know, are masters of their laws,
> And may resolve them to what forms they please,
> So all conclude in justice.[51]

The die has been cast; Chapman has at some length debated the two sides of the issue—the old idea of the established order with the King at the head and the new idea of the freedom of the individual of which Byron is the example. His decision to support the former, devoting the last act to Byron's struggle to avoid his death, is made the more poignant by Henry's appeal to God as the final action is set in motion:

> O Thou that govern'st the keen swords of kings,
> Direct my arm in this important stroke,
> Or hold it being advanc'd.[52]

Early in *The Conspiracy,* Byron soliloquizes that if he is "burst" like the shaft of Hercules,

> in my heart
> This shall be written: "Yet 'twas high and right."[53]

For nine acts Chapman then weighs in careful fashion the two courses that the lives of Henry and Byron represent, deciding whether the sovereign or the subject has the greater right. The conclusion he draws in refusing to permit Byron to go free after two conspiracies against the Crown is a Stoic one which Byron himself inadvertently drew when D'Aumale was exiled to Brussels:

> So, when men fly the natural clime of truth,
> And turn themselves loose out of all the bounds
> Of justice and the straight way to their ends,
> Forsaking all the sure force in themselves
> To seek without them that which is not theirs,
> The forms of all their comforts are distracted,
> The riches of their freedoms forfeited,
> Their human noblesse sham'd, the mansions
> Of their cold spirits eaten down with cares,
> And all their ornaments of wit and valour,
> Learning, and judgment, cut from all their fruits.[54]

We are forced to conclude that Chapman came to regard Byron's actions as neither high nor right.

The fifth act of *The Tragedy* is chiefly interesting for the dramatic power it attains in telling the story of Byron's reaction to the death sentence and for the form the story takes.[55] In this final act we find a carefully reiterated motif—the fulfillment of the death sentence may yet be averted if Byron will but throw himself on the mercy of the King. But while this theme dominates Act V, it has nevertheless appeared in both *The Conspiracy* and the earlier acts of *The Tragedy,* as if Chapman with a deliberate casualness had dropped hints along the way of the manner in which the tragedy was at last to be revealed; then with telling effect he directs the action that fills the time between the death sentence and its execution to various moments of suspense that derive their effect from the opportunities given Byron to save his life and his soul.

In *The Tragedy,* the audience is again theatened with the possibility that Byron may escape retribution by submitting as he had done at the end of *The Conspiracy.* In the third scene of Act I, Henry promises, "Yet on submission, I vow still his pardon."[56] Tragedy may yet be averted. The second act, composed of only one scene in the present arrangement of the existing text, contains no material that affects the action of the play in any way, but in Scene 2 of Act III, Henry is again explicit in promising pardon to Byron upon his return to Court—

> Always reserving clemency and pardon
> Upon confession, be you ne'er so foul.[57]

In their promise of clemency, these references point toward the later use that Chapman makes of the "mercy" theme; "if" Byron will only confess, there will be no demand for justice. Soissons states the matter clearly to Byron in Scene I of Act IV:

> My lord, if you respect your name and race,
> The preservation of your former honours,
> Merits, and virtues, humbly cast them all
> At the King's mercy;[58]

but Byron does not again yield as he did at the close of *The Conspiracy*, thereby prompting Henry in Scene 2 to ask,

> What shall we do with this unthankful man?
> Would he of one thing but reveal the truth,
> Which I have proof of, underneath his hand,
> He should not taste my justice.[59]

Henry makes one final plea to save Byron, of whom he has already said, "I never lov'd man like him."[60] He turns to him in the closing passages of the final scene of Act IV, with his last offer:

>   yet is your will resolved
> To duty and the main bond of your life?
> I swear, of all th' intrusions I have made
> Upon your own good and continu'd fortunes,
> This is the last; inform me yet the truth,
> And here I vow to you (by all my love,
> By all means shown you even to this extreme,
> When all men else forsake you) you are safe.[61]

But as Byron replies, "This nail is driven already past the head,"[62] and, as the conspirators are led away under guard, Epernon concludes the act with a basically Stoic statement:

>   his state still is best
> That hath most inward worth; and that's best tried
> That neither glories, nor is glorified.[63]

Before the drama of Byron's fall is resumed in Scene 3 of Act IV, the mental background against which the action is to be played is carefully set. The topic of the proper relation between king and subject is reviewed with marked emphasis upon the King's position as the cause of right. Against this backdrop, we hear that Byron's attitude is one befitting Bussy—

> he disdains
> To grace the prison with the slend'rest show
> Of any patience,[64]

and like Bussy, too, "He breathes defiance to the world."[65] The second scene of Act V shows Byron fighting in a court of law for his life, answering the Chancellor's charges with virtuous indignation if not with conviction, and defending himself with haughty superiority. He counters the charges by asking, as the Renaissance individualist,

> What man is he
> That is so high but he would higher be?[66]

He gives as a cause of his fall, "I did deserve too much,"[67] and calls attention to his own worth by stating as a principle of ethics,

> Virtue in great men must be small and slight,
> For poor stars rule where she is exquisite.[68]

And he wards off any attack on his "intemperate speech"—"But reason ever did my deeds attend."[69] Byron's defense, however, is discarded, and, when the Chancellor finally decides,

> Time was the cause, not will; the mind's free act
> In treason still is judg'd as th' outward fact,[70]

legal opinion has added dignity to Henry's position, and we know for certain that Byron's cause has really been lost from the start, that he must die.[71]

The dramatic account of Byron's reactions to that decision is resumed in Scene 3; at first, Byron refuses to be intimidated, asking like a Stoic,

> Is't it possible the King should be so vain
> To think he can shake me with *fear of death?*
> Or make me apprehend that he intends it?[72]

But when the Chancellor and his followers come to his cell "in the Bastille" to pronounce sentence, Byron has softened a little, and his question, "Is there no pardon, will there come no mercy?"[73] while not completely dispelling the doubt of the outcome, is nonetheless touched with despair. He remembers,

>   the Queen of England
> Told me that if the wilful Earl of Essex
> Had us'd submission, and but ask'd her mercy,
> She would have given it past resumption. . . .
> He still refus'd grace, I importune it.[74]

At this point, Chapman, having reduced Byron to importuning for grace, permits him again to retrieve a remnant of his former individualism and glory. And, although no sense of dramatic struggle develops from this interlude which precedes the relentless march of his destiny, yet *The Tragedy* does gain dramatic intensity from the interruption typified by Byron's saying, "I'll break my blood's high billows 'gainst my stars."[75] Then, too, Byron's attitude towards death in this scene, with its overtones of Stoicism, is reminiscent of Bussy's at a similar time. Advised by the Bishop to prepare to die, Byron counters,

> Horror of death! Let me alone in peace.
> And leave my soul to me, whom it concerns;
> You have no charge of it; I feel her free.[76]

He knows as well as Bussy,

> this body [is] but a sink of folly . . .
> A slave bound face to face to Death till death,[77]

that

> life is but a dark and stormy night . . .
> And Death is nothing;[78]

and like Bussy he will face death bravely,

> like the captain
> That pray'd on horseback, and with sword in hand,
> Threaten'd the sun, commanding it to stand;
> These are but ropes of sand.[79]

And believing

> for one fault,
> I forfeit all the fashion of a man,[80]

Byron even surpasses the Stoics in stating,

> O happy were the man could live alone,
> To know no man, nor be of any known![81]

and in realizing,

> He is at no end of his actions blest
> Whose ends will make him greatest, and not best.[82]

But Chapman does not permit Byron to die at this most manly of his moments, for, when Vitry asks him at the end of his farewell to the world to mount the scaffold, Byron indicates that his heart and his mind are not of one accord: "Not a breath/ Of any mercy yet?"[83] And when the hangman tells him to kneel, Byron cries out, "Hold, stay a little! Comes there yet no mercy?"[84] Only then, when the possibility of a reprieve has been exhausted and retribution must come, can Byron admit to what may well pass for his epitaph, the moral to which his life is hostage, "And kings' suspicions needs no balances."[85]

A detailed analysis of the way in which Chapman has presented the protagonist's repeated appeal to mercy has been necessary to make clear the basic distinction between the final consummation of the tragedy in the last act and the form of its presentation. It may very well be that Byron's vacillation between Stoicism and his hope for mercy is Chapman's attempt to present his fall in terms of tragedy. But, as Spencer rightly points out, "Byron, whose protest against death and the platitudes of the Middle Ages is so typical of the time, comes to an imperfect end because of the defects which are inherent in his egotistical point of view";[86] yet neither Spencer nor any other critic has considered the equally important fact that Chapman followed the technique of an English tragedy of the Middle Ages in postponing the demands of justice that eventually culminate in Byron's death: the device of defeating justice through an appeal to mercy. In *The Medieval Heritage of Elizabethan Tragedy,* Farnham discusses[87] the English morality play, *The Castle of Perseverance,* observing that "bound for Hell," Mankind in his last words calls "upon God for mercy."[88] While mercy exceeds justice in this and other moralities, it is dominated by the law of justice in Byron's tragedy. Farnham's contention that "so long as the moral dramatist and his audience conceive that a universal law of justice, under which man lives and engages himself with destiny, is dominated by the force of mercy, their recognition of tragedy must necessarily be small"[89] bears directly on the tragic significance of this drama. For, although the story appears in Chapman's source much as it does in the two plays, with Byron's making one confession but refusing to make a second, the fact remains that Chapman's pointing up for dramatic purposes the just death that comes to Byron shows his mind repeating in the ten acts of Byron's story the whole development of tragedy in the old morality plays. That justice had become one of the ends of tragedy is clearly indicated, for, regardless of Byron's end in the source work, that end had become the only possible one in the tragedy that bears his name. In the English tragedy of 1607-08, mercy no longer dared temper justice. Nor is it necessary to suggest that Chapman knew *The Castle of Perseverance* (*ca.* 1425) since the outline of his play existed in his source; but it is interesting to note that in 1607-08, almost two hundred years later than this morality, the history of English tragedy was duplicated in Chapman's great tragic epic. In discussing the history of that development as revealed in this one morality play, Farnham states that "this shift in balance [from mercy to justice] has as much bearing upon the development of tragedy as the shift from Fortune to retribution in *De Casibus* narrative."[90]

Again, we find that Chapman has had to experiment throughout the play to achieve a goal that had long been a part of English tragedy. We have seen in *Bussy D'Ambois* that Chapman swings in the course of those five acts from Fortune to Destiny to explain Bussy's tragedy. And while retribution, as Farnham uses the word, cannot be made synonymous with Chapman's conception of Destiny, the dramatist nevertheless uses Destiny to make a necessary explanation of what befalls Bussy, the retribution that death demands from him who flaunts and violates the ethical code. In his second and third tragical dramas about Byron, Chapman again emphasizes this moral principle.

The two Byron plays indicate that Chapman's technique as a writer of tragedy was surer than we found it in *Bussy D'Ambois*. The subject matter has become more unified in that Chapman confines his second epic tragedy to the exposition of a single idea—the moral obligation of the subject to his king, an obligation that Chapman concludes must remain inviolate if social chaos is to be averted. Byron, whom Chapman uses for the demonstration of this thesis, emerges in his defeat as a figure whose association with Bussy becomes a matter of necessity; they are conceived in the same mold, appearing, like Hotspur, as young, hot-blooded, impetuous men of action, though in both cases we witness the results of their actions rather than the actions themselves.[91] In form, too, Chapman has developed his art as he writes about Byron. Singleness of idea leads to singleness of technique, for there are few irrevelant crosscurrents in either *The Conspiracy* or *The Tragedy*, as there are in *Bussy*.

Chapman's limiting his exposition to a single theme developed with singleness of purpose naturally results in a drama of sharper focus but narrower scope than *Bussy D'Ambois;* in the narrowness of *Bussy* lies the explanation of its greater appeal, for, though it is not as technically sound as the two *Byron* plays, yet its all-inclusiveness at times gives it great power—it is "good theater," as the succeeding plays are not. In the story of Byron there is a sameness that even the intensity of the telling does not relieve, a sameness that extends to the characters who create Byron's drama as well as to the theme. With the exception of the three Ladies of the Court who appear only in the last part of the final scene of *The Conspiracy,* we move in a masculine world in which women have no place. Their absence is both striking and significant.

And yet despite their narrow scope, these two plays contain several of those very qualities that constitute both the tragic effectiveness of Bussy and the dramatic power of Chapman at his artistic peak. In the first place, the irrational conflict of man against the world so typical of Bussy still obtains in Byron. Though the latter may on occasion try to persuade us that his actions proceed from reasoned deliberation, he achieves little more than a rationalization of actions intrinsically comparable to Bussy's emotional outbursts. As a result, he, too, emerges as the Renaissance hero whose selfish aims threaten the world with the same moral chaos as Bussy's egomania engenders. At the same time, however, Chapman has relegated Byron to a more limited society than that in which Bussy moves. Bussy numbers among his friends both King and pretender, both men and women; he is praised by those who accept him and tolerated by those who fear him. He chooses to run with the hare and hunt with the hounds. The story of his life is dramatic to the extent that he recognizes no human limitation. But Chapman has created Byron in a less tolerant mood. The King will forgive Byron if he will reform. Barring that, the King will sacrifice him to his own ideal of the State. When the treacherous La Fin at last betrays Byron in order to give his allegiance to his King, Byron stands alone, condemned in his defeat. For that very reason, Byron's attitude toward approaching death never achieves the glory that attends Bussy at a like time, for his death has been dictated as much by moral strictures as by the inevitable demands of Destiny. *Good* as represented by Henry's sovereignty simply triumphs over *evil* as typified by Byron's treachery.

An appreciation of the marked difference between these two points of view is crucial to an appraisal of the place occupied by the *Byron* plays in the development of Chapman's artistry in tragedy. For in other respects the Stoic influences here at work do not differ greatly from those affecting the outcome of *Bussy D'Ambois;* in both instances, Chapman's use of Stoic doctrine does not go very far beyond the conventional level with the important exception of the character of the King in the *Byron* plays. In this one role Chapman has fashioned a character who clearly reflects his indebtedness to Stoic ideology. The King's position as God's representative with the authority to condemn to death a false subject on highly ethical principles should give Byron's fall greater tragic significance. In reality, however, that fall achieves only the semblance of tragedy because Byron has been denied the right to oppose the King. Byron must fall—right must prevail; Bussy, too, must fall—but not solely because of any moral issue between right and wrong, good and evil. Bussy's tragic flaw is that he initiates a train of actions he is powerless to control. Byron's is that the major premise of his conduct, " 'Tis immortality to die aspiring,"[92] is as unreasonable as the aspiration and pride which feed it; no amount of reasoning can then justify what Janin calls "the fatal thirst of his ambition."[93]

As a result, Chapman's inclination towards Stoicism therefore appears in a stronger light in *The Conspiracy and Tragedy of Charles Duke of Byron.* In *Bussy D'Ambois,* this inclination is a thing we discern as from afar, for the play contains no character against which that of Bussy is clearly contrasted. His King never achieves a thorough individuality—at the height of Bussy's daring effrontery to Monsieur, for instance, the King steps forth to protect him, to lead him from the stage to "covert."[94] At this point, midway in Scene 1 of Act IV, Henry leaves the stage and does not reappear. We can only infer that Bussy's actions are acceptable in the King's sight. But the King Henry of the *Byron* plays is no such unpredictable ruler. He stands staunchly at the head of his people,[95] as their protector under God's will. In such a man, Chapman has depicted a great ruler who achieves kingship in every sense of the word through his refusal to be deposed by a man of lesser moral stature. In his King, Byron meets an antagonist who almost develops into the protagonist. And while Henry is no Stoical man such as Chabot, for example, he is the epitome of Stoic doctrine in that he represents the Stoic's desire to see Nature, as the manifestation of God's will, maintained. By the very fact that he takes precedence over Byron, Henry personifies the kind of man whom Chapman's reasonable mind at last approved.

Just as the tragedy of Bussy is, in the final analysis, no tragedy at all, so there is no true tragedy in Byron. We may at times regret that such a man, possessing elements of decided greatness, finds it impossible to direct his powers toward some cause worthy of his ability. But his fall, predicated on invalid issues by which our sympathies are never touched, robs him of the qualities of a moving tragic protagonist. Even if Byron is saved by confessing his treason to the King, the cause he represents must still fail, not because of any rule of dramatic propriety, but rather because it is not man's right to succeed ultimately in a fight that is ethically unsound. Byron never has a chance to win; we must, therefore, watch an action incapable of stirring our sensibilities beyond an admiration for Chapman's attempt to give it dramatic vitality.

Since the nature of Byron's flaw places him nearer Bussy than Clermont,[96] the ten acts to which Byron gives his name must be regarded as the transition between *Bussy* and *The Revenge of Bussy*, revealing the extent to which the philosophy of Stoicism was more and more shaping Chapman's thinking and art.

CHAPTER THREE: THE REVENGE
OF BUSSY D'AMBOIS

And for the autentical truth of either person or action, who (worth the respecting) will expect it in a
poem, whose subject is not truth, but things like
truth? Poor envious souls they are that cavil at truth's
want in these natural fictions: material instruction,
elegant and sententious excitation to virtue, and deflection from her contrary, being the soul, limbs, and
limits of an autentical tragedy.

Dedication to Sir Thomas Howard,
The Revenge of Bussy D'Ambois.

IN *Bussy D'Ambois* and *The Conspiracy and Tragedy of Byron,*
Chapman reveals an interest in and a susceptibility to Stoicism. In
The Revenge of Bussy D'Ambois he has *become* a Stoic.

As Chapman wrote *The Revenge of Bussy D'Ambois,* late in
1610, or in 1611,[1] fulfilling the promise of a sequel made in the
"Epilogue" to the first *Bussy* play, his growing interest in Stoicism
dominated almost every line. Since this strong Stoic influence appears as early as 1610-11, Miss Bartlett may postpone the date un-
necessarily when she asserts that Epictetus "was Chapman's most
important reading in the years 1611-12."[2] Chapman must have
begun a careful, serious reading of Epictetus even before he began
writing *The Revenge,* for, when he wrote this play, he had become
a "convert" to the philosophy that pervades it. Passages from the
Discourses now begin to make their appearance with some regularity, as if Chapman's reading so filled his mind that the play became a Stoic commentary upon French history, to which the dramatist had again turned for his subject matter. Indeed, *The Revenge
of Bussy,* apart from its revenge theme, is little more than an anal-

ysis of the tenets of Stoicism on both the general and specific levels. Sometimes this analysis has distinct bearing upon the revenge-tragedy which this play purports to be; more often the drama assumes an episodic quality, simply coming to a halt while Chapman through Clermont examines a particular Stoic doctrine that impresses him at the moment, but which does not become an integral part of the action.

As a result, *The Revenge* from the Dedication forward is conceived on a highly ethical plane. In the Dedication to Sir Thomas Howard, Chapman states his conception of tragedy: "Material instruction, elegant and sententious excitation to virtue, and deflection from her contrary, being the soul, limbs, and limits of an autentical tragedy,"[3] a definition with which any one of his Stoic teachers would probably have agreed. Indeed, when in Scene 1 of Act I Clermont, the Guise, and Baligny discuss the world as a stage, Clermont quotes Epictetus, "the good Greek moralist,"[4] to substantiate his claim that the stage is to be respected because of the didactic powers of the actor, whatever the role. Then, too, just as in the last sonnet comprising "A Coronet for his mistress Philosophie" (1595) Chapman praised the theaters of Athens and of Rome because they showed

> theyr glories there
> To noblest wits, and men of highest doome,
> That for the kingly Lawrell bent affayre;[5]

so the Guise, condemning those who seek material things and disregard man, God's own "temple,"[6] says

> I would have these things
> Brought upon stages, to let mighty misers
> See all their grave and serious miseries play'd,
> As once they were in Athens and old Rome.[7]

The Guise himself calls Clermont's criticism of Democritus, "the splenative philosopher"[8] who went to the theater to laugh at everything, a "virtuous digression"; and it is this very kind of digression, so common in *The Revenge,* that emphasizes the ethical character of the play.

But Chapman was supposedly not composing a treatise on Stoic ethics; he was writing what the title page of the published play termed "A Tragedie."[9] His technique in dramatic tragedy had failed, however, to keep pace with his growing interest in Stoicism; the result was that Chapman gave less attention to the form of the revenge-tragedy than to ethical problems that had patently become his chief concern. Chapman's eagerness to capitalize on "box office appeal" was simply sacrificed to the stronger urge of presenting his first full-length portrait of the Stoical man. That the revenge theme was, nevertheless, of some importance to Chapman as he conceived his play may be seen in the fact that in his source "there was neither revenger nor revenge for the murder of Bussy";[10] furthermore, "Clermont D'Ambois cannot be identified with any historical character."[11] And we shall see that Chapman's creation of Clermont to serve as "his ideal figure of the revenger"[12] raised problems he found difficult to solve, for the revenge motif failed to hold his interest as he developed scene after scene of the tragedy.

Although the first act of *The Revenge* deals with the initial plotting of Bussy's revenge, the second entirely neglects this theme with the exception of the reference by Baligny, who tells Clermont that he must pass some time at Cambrai while waiting for Tamyra and Lord Renel to plan for Clermont's "sworn wreak"[13] on Montsurry. The third act reveals the working out of Henry's and Baligny's plot to capture Clermont, with Charlotte and Clermont making only occasional references to revenge. Not until the first scene of Act V is the subject of the actual revenge resumed; then, Bussy's Umbra rises to urge it; a short second scene shows Henry plotting the Guise's death because the Guise forced "D'Ambois'

freedom." Bussy's ghost again urges his revenge in Scene 3, while
Scene 4 is given over to the Guise's murder. In Scene 5 Clermont
finally dispatches Montsurry, and the revenge which the play has
thus far successfully avoided at last becomes a *fait accompli*. But
Montsurry's death is not permitted to become the supreme catastrophe of *The Revenge:* that place of honor is reserved for Clermont's suicide, which brings the dramatic action to a close. Clermont's suicide in itself introduces a significant departure from the
technique of the usual revenge-tragedy, but the fact that so few
scenes throughout the five acts actually treat the subject which purports to be the theme of the tragedy is equally significant. The
scenes that constitute the bulk of the play are either wholly unrelated to Bussy's revenge or are given over to long speeches in which
it is treated only incidentally. Whereas in *Hamlet* the entire dramatic action bears upon Hamlet's final avenging his father's murder
despite a number of delays, *The Revenge* often appears to be a
series of unrelated soliloquies and episodes that are important only
in so far as they reveal Chapman's interest in Clermont, a Stoical
man. Even in the scenes in which revenge is the chief topic, the
lines are interesting chiefly because of their concern with the Stoical
character of Clermont, for this reflective man has now come to
dominate Chapman's mind more completely than Bussy or Byron
ever had done.

The very first lines of *The Revenge* suggest the fact that Chapman intends to apply the ethical standards outlined in the Dedication; they are even made to apply to the first Bussy play, and they
establish to a certain extent the tone of its sequel:

> To what will this declining kingdom turn,
> Swinging in every license, as in this
> Stupid permission of brave D'Ambois' murther?
> Murther made parallel with law![14]

One cannot help being surprised that there is greater concern over Bussy's murder than over Bussy's killing of Barrisor, L'Anou, and Pyrhot; it is impossible to justify their deaths since these men were at least innocent of breaking the moral law. But Chapman's interest in the laws by which kings and their subjects must live in the social order had increased, and, as we shall see, the dramatist had become dissatisfied with Bussy's assumption that he was a law unto himself. Now the dramatist wished to investigate further Henry's role of God's Sovereign in the *Byron* plays. The problem continued to interest Chapman in both of his later tragedies, too; but in *The Revenge* he gave it his fullest attention.

A reference in Scene 1 of Act II emphatically establishes Clermont as an ethical man in contrast to Bussy. The Guise compares them:

He [Clermont] hath the crown of man, and all his parts,
Which learning is; and that so true and virtuous
That it gives power to do as well as say
Whatever fits a most accomplish'd man;
Which Bussy, for his valour's season, lack'd;
And was so rapt with outrage oftentimes
Beyond decorum;[15]

The Stoical bent of Chapman's mind as he wrote *The Revenge* is perfectly shown in these lines that not only repudiate the character who once called forth his sympathy, but also create the world of "decorum" synonymous with the ethics of Stoicism. The implication is at once evident: Clermont will not go "beyond decorum."

Although the Stoics all placed their greatest emphasis upon the important role Reason must play in a man's life, Chapman's treatment of Clermont more often implies than explicitly states its importance. In the full-length picture of Clermont that the Guise gives in the fourth scene of Act IV, the word "reason" nowhere appears; Clermont's actions, however, are always in full accord

with that Stoic doctrine. The one time he does choose openly to defend Reason occurs in connection with Bussy's revenge, which
Charlotte, Bussy's sister and Baligny's wife, urges him to exact. Not
satisfied with the slowness of that revenge, she objects to Clermont's "noble course"[16] in sending a challenge. If, as Parrott believes, Clermont represents Chapman's ideal figure of the revenger,[17] then Stoicism has taken full possession of the dramatist's
mind, for Clermont parries Charlotte's objections by asking, "Shall
we revenge a villany with villany?"[18] Such an ethical approach to
the subject of revenge is an entirely new conception in the revenge-
tragedy, for heretofore revenge had been conceived in terms of
emotion rather than of reason. Charlotte's reaction follows the pattern expected in a play of this genre—villainy must be repaid with
villainy. But Clermont objects:

> Shall we equal be
> With villains? Is that your reason?
> *Char.*   Cowardice evermore
> Flies to the shield of reason.
> *Cler.*   Nought that is
> Approv'd by reason can be cowardice.[19]

Obviously, Clermont's indecision is in no way comparable to
Hamlet's. Clermont's delay is in reality no delay at all since his
reason has for the time being stifled within him the desire for revenge:

> I repent that ever
> (By any instigation in th' appearance
> My brother's spirit made, as I imagin'd)
> That e'er I yielded to revenge his murther.
> All worthy men should ever bring their blood
> To bear all ill, not to be wreak'd with good:
> Do ill for no ill; never private cause
> Should take on it the part of public laws.[20]

Perhaps nothing could so fully measure the distance between Clermont and Bussy as the final lines of this passage, for, while Bussy believes that he can justify taking the law into his own hands, Clermont holds the very antithesis of this belief: man is not justified in usurping the function of "public law."

The fact that Clermont must finally avenge Bussy in no way militates against this conclusion since Reason, as well as Bussy's Ghost, dictates the action. Bussy's sister, Charlotte, married Baligny only on the condition that he should do everything possible to avenge the murder of her brother.[21] But, as Clermont explains the matter to the Guise,[22] Bussy's Ghost cannot accept Baligny as his avenger in view of his treachery. Hence, literally against his will, Clermont's reason must accept the Ghost's ultimatum: "Clermont must author this just tragedy."[23] Consequently, the most powerful section of *The Revenge,* that part of Scene 5, Act V, devoted to Clermont's killing of Montsurry, does not detract from the Stoical man's reliance upon his reason, and the accomplishment of Bussy's revenge becomes the logical and inevitable conclusion of Clermont's duty, which Reason alone has prescribed.

Chapman's devotion to the Stoic doctrine of Reason makes another appearance in *The Revenge* in a somewhat strange connection —Clermont's reasoned defense of the Guise's part in the Massacre of St. Bartholomew's Day, 1572. The playwright's interest in this historical event had been demonstrated earlier in *Byron's Tragedy.* There, Henry at one point questions whether or not Byron's renewed associations with the conspirators

> Are . . . proofs of that purely Catholic zeal
> That made him wish no other glorious title
> Than to be call'd the Scourge of Huguenots?[24]

Professor Parrott notes that these lines have their parallel in Grimeston's *General Inventory,* Chapman's source, and advances the theory that Byron's "zeal against the Huguenots was apparently a mere cloak to conceal his ambitious designs, and to unite him more closely with such bigoted Catholics as Fuentes and the Duke of Savoy."[25] Since Chapman was drawing a sympathtic portrait of Byron, this zeal may be considered a natural characteristic of a thoroughly non-Stoical protagonist rather than an indication of Chapman's personal sympathies. But other references in *Byron's Tragedy* seem to denote a pro-Catholic bent in Chapman, for Byron refers without criticism from the dramatist to "all the Catholic Princes' aids"[26] with whom he has joined. Byron defends Alexander the Great as a king who sought religion[27] rather than "gold and empire,"[28] who desired to

> Extend religion through it [his empire], and all nations
> Reduce to one firm constitution
> Of piety, justice, and one public weal;
> To which end he made all his matchless subjects
> Make tents their castles and their garrisons;
> True Catholics, countrymen and their allies;[29]

Byron even attributes his fall to the fact that he is a "good" Catholic, and Janin's report

> That . . . he never wish'd more glorious title
> Than to be call'd the Scourge of Huguenots[30]

recalls Henry's previous statement to the same effect.

Whether or not Chapman's presentation of Byron's conspiracy indicates his sympathy with the Catholic cause, the fact remains that Byron's zeal is in no way out of harmony with Chapman's portrait of him; it may be judged a fitting attribute of the man who will use every opportunity to realize his ambition.

Clermont's defense of the Guise, however, cannot be so easily dismissed: it springs from the character of a man whose Stoical

qualities Chapman patently approves, even though the two references to Catholicism in *The Revenge* are not altogether consistent.
On the first occasion, Baligny asserts that "the Massacre" is a blem-
ish that "sticks by him [the Guise] still."[31] And to Baligny's description of the Guise's part in it as heinous, Clermont counters,

> To a brutish sense,
> But not a manly reason.[32]

To Clermont, as might be expected, the real slaughter lay in the
corruption of truth, which the Massacre sought to destroy:

> This is the beastly slaughter made of men,
> When truth is overthrown, his laws corrupted;
> When souls are smother'd in the flatter'd flesh,
> Slain bodies are no more than oxen slain.[33]

The only distinction Clermont will permit Baligny to make between men and oxen lies in the difference of "their communities of
faith and reason,"[34] and he concludes,

> Had faith and true religion been preferr'd,
> Religious Guise had never massacred.[35]

If this remained the only occasion in *The Revenge* on which Chapman referred to the Guise's participation in the famous Massacre,
we should be forced to conclude that he fully realized the wide
discrepancy existing between the Guise of *Bussy D'Ambois,* a man
leagued with Monsieur against the established order and the laws
of decency, and the Guise of *The Revenge,* Clermont's alter ego.
Having so completely changed the conception of the Guise in the
second *Bussy* play and made Clermont the Guise's tutor in Stoic
doctrines, Chapman had to justify his devotion to a man whose
moral code the audience had every right to question. Clermont's
own position of respect was thus maintained with the audience at

the same time that the Guise was raised to a level on which his fit-
ness as Clermont's friend was logically established.

Yet a later reference to the Guise's continued interest in the
"propagation of the Catholic cause"[36] leads us to question the extent of Chapman's Catholic sympathies, for Clermont cautions his
friend against continuing in the plot:

> Let all fall that would rise unlawfully:
> Make not your forward spirit in virtue's right
> A property for vice, by thrusting on
> Further than all your powers can fetch you off.
> It is enough, your will is infinite
> To all things virtuous and religious,
> Which, within limits kept, may without danger
> Let virtue some good from your graces gather.[37]

Whatever Chapman's real religious sympathies were, then, he
nevertheless achieves in *The Revenge* an artistic symmetry by re-
trieving the Guise's reputation, already damaged in *Bussy,* at the
same time that he intimates, through the character of Clermont,
that Byron had favored Catholicism not because of his religious
convictions but because of his desire for personal aggrandizement.

Clermont, like the ideal Stoical man, was wise and virtuous, too.
Early in the play, at a time when Renel and Baligny are discussing
the world's falling away from virtue, Renel stresses the importance
of the wise man to society. Ignorance is presented as the reason for
the corruption of man's first nature,[38] since ignorance leads to idle-
ness and

> idle men
> Most practise what they most may do with ease,
> Fashion, and favour; all their studies aiming
> At getting money, which no wise man ever
> Fed his desires with.[39]

Bussy was exactly that kind of man; by contrast Clermont appears "truly wise," possessing a trait "which all men else despise."

Monsieur regards Clermont as one

> Holding all learning but an art to live well,
> And showing he hath learn'd it in his life,
> Being thereby strong in his persuading others.[40]

The Guise, too, believes

> He hath the crown of man, and all his parts,
> Which learning is;[41]

but he adds a qualification:

> and for his rare learning,
> He is not (as all else are that seek knowledge)
> Of taste so much deprav'd, that they had rather
> Delight, and satisfy themselves to drink
> Of the stream troubled, wand'ring ne'er so far
> From the clear fount, than of the fount itself.
> In all, Rome's Brutus is reviv'd in him,
> Whom he of industry doth imitate.[42]

Clermont himself has a high opinion of the place of wisdom and the uses to which it should be put, his words incidentally substantiating Renel's belief that ignorance is at the core of a decadent social structure:

> So our wit's sharpness, which we should employ
> In noblest knowledge, we should never waste
> In vile and vulgar admirations.[43]

This contempt for "vile and vulgar admirations," based on the right use of learning, is of a piece with Chapman's professed hatred for "the prophane multitude" expressed in the Dedication of *Ovid's Banqvet of Sence,* "TO THE TRVLIE Learned, and my worthy

Friende, Ma. *Mathew Royden,*"[44] and in his *Ivstification of Andromeda Liberata,* "*Learning* hath delighted from her Cradle to hide her selfe from the base and prophane *Vulgare,* her ancient Enemy."[45] This intellectual snobbery is a part of Chapman's resentment of the fact that in government the virtuous man was often victimized by the opportunist without moral scruples. Chapman's principles were never democratic—his ideal world was one in which virtuous wise men controlled the government and administered its laws. He knew that though good men might be poor, they must be bound together in an aristocracy of mental superiority. Chapman seems not to have remembered, however, Marcus Aurelius' insistence that a good man has duties to his fellow men, regardless of their minds or social positions.

Clermont's adherence to ethical principles and his reliance on Reason make the Guise's description of him as one "rightly to virtue fram'd"[46] all the more significant; Chapman devotes many lines of *The Revenge* to an exhibition of Clermont's virtue. As if to underline this virtue, Chapman expresses the belief that the world of which he is writing has fallen away from virtue because men now emphasize unimportant things. In the second speech of the play, Renel states that when kings fell prey to pride, "Virtue quite was vanish'd."[47] His praise of the good old days results in a conversation with Baligny marking the difference between "now" and "then" and ending in a defense of war, which "then" permitted virtue to triumph.

Monsieur, however, seems quite content with his world, for he vents his spleen on the Guise and Clermont, stating that Clermont's opinion of his own virtues has persuaded the Guise that in embracing these virtues he is "embracing him." From this point forward, the play belongs to the Guise and to Clermont, for they are the two characters who reveal not only the lack of virtue in others but the disreputable state of the world as well. They are the men who

> Devour each other with . . . virtue's zeal,
> And leave for other friends no fragment:[48]

who tempt Baligny to comment in contempt,

> So these, out of an unseen good in virtue,
> Make arguments of right and comfort in her,
> That clothe them like the poor web of a spinner.[49]

Again, it is three of the King's men, Aumale, Chalon, and Maillard, who cannot understand that Clermont's pursuit of virtue brings him a happiness which the life of the Court does not permit. Aumale, for example, expresses surprise that Clermont with "so sure a foot in virtue"[50] should incur the King's displeasure; Maillard answers that

> To keep her [virtue] low, and in her proper place;
> Height hath no room for her. . . .
> So, let one marry this same barren Virtue,
> She never lets him rest, where fruitful Vice
> Spares her rich drudge, gives him in labour breath,
> Feeds him with bane, and makes him fat with death.[51]

But Clermont realizes that virtue must never be made the sole reason for man's advancement. Bussy could accept with his mind the belief that unless one was guided by virtue, no place was secure; but, dissatisfied with virtue's slow pace, he was all too willing to trust to Fortune's favors. Charlotte may accuse Clermont of speaking "all principle,"[52] but he will abide by his principles: though virtue for virtue's sake was not enough for Bussy, it suffices for Clermont. He can therefore advise the Guise to retire from the plot to advance the Catholic faith, as we have noted, since it necessitates his going contrary to virtue. And in the lines bearing his advice, he effectively contradicts Maillard's denunciation of virtue and choice of "fruitful Vice."

Clermont's uncompromising reliance on the principle of virtuous living characterizes him as a man shaped by Stoical doctrine. One is tempted to believe that this idealized portrait of Clermont, a man without historical antecedent, represents Chapman's determination to present his own views of the world about him through a fictitious character of French history. If so, Clermont is an indication that the author of *The Revenge* was finding solace, as the founders of Stoicism found it in the establishment of certain ideals, in the creation of a portrait reflecting his own search for security. Like Clermont, Chapman because of his inability to win the independence he so earnestly desired must have been often forced to rely largely upon abstract principles in devising conduct that would most effectively accept the challenge of events; the philosophy of Stoicism offered him decided moral support.

Chapman seems to have been less concerned with the Stoic concept of Nature in *The Revenge* than in the earlier tragedies. The reason is that he has made the entire action of the play conform to the demands of Nature more than in his earlier plays. In *The Revenge,* there is no Bussy or Byron to oppose God's will—Clermont at no time threatens to violate Nature's plan. It would be proper, then, if the occasional references to Nature appeared only as Clermont and the Guise deviated from their predestined courses. In the first scene of Act V, the Umbra Bussy arises to occupy the stage alone—in Simpson's words "the most philosophic Ghost in Elizabethan drama."[53] Although the Ghost appears ostensibly "to urge . . . justice,"[54] he nevertheless indulges in philosophical reflection that bears only the slightest relationship to his demand for revenge. It is indeed strange to find Bussy's Ghost moralizing on good and evil men when he had so boldly ignored the distinction before his death. Now he tells the audience

> That all the joints and nerves sustaining nature
> As well may break, and yet the world abide,

> As any one good unrewarded die,
> Or any one ill scape his penalty.[55]

Although his logic is questionable, since it can be argued that Bussy's death was a just penalty for his sins as well as that his death left "good unrewarded," we cannot fail to be impressed by this Ghost's knowledge. Somewhere between life and death he has learned that the world cannot endure if Nature's supporting joints and nerves are destroyed.

Clermont's later reference to Nature, in the same scene, is noteworthy for its emphasis upon the "temperate appetite," a phrase which has wider implications than the literal interpretation of the word "appetite" would at first indicate. In one of his tutorial sessions with his Stoical pupil, Clermont tells the Guise,

> for as when only Nature
> Moves men to meat, as far as her power rules,
> She doth it with a temperate appetite,
> The too much men devour abhorring Nature;
> And in our most health is our most disease.[56]

We cannot help thinking that "the too much men" were Bussy and Byron, the two whose appetites for power and position caused their fall. In their attempts to depose Nature, they were in turn deposed. Chapman points to Clermont, however, as one who knows that man cannot overthrow her with impunity.

Clermont's refusal to associate with diseased mankind is further illustrated by his personal devotion to the Universal Being whose will the Stoics made one with Nature while insisting that man contained within him a spark of the divine essence. Clermont further recognizes the Stoic doctrine that Nature has created each man for some particular purpose. Chapman places all these related ideas together in one speech, adapted from Epictetus, in which Clermont deliberates with Renel upon the consequences of falling into the King's trap:

> he, that knowing how divine a frame
> The whole world is; and of it all, can name
> (Without self-flattery) no part so divine
> As he himself, and therefore will confine
> Freely his whole powers in his proper part,
> Goes on most God-like. He that strives t'invert
> The Universal's course with his poor way,
> Not only dust-like shivers with the sway,
> But, crossing God in his great work, all earth
> Bears not so cursed and so damn'd a birth.[57]

And when Clermont is finally seized, he signalizes his absolute acceptance of whatever the Universal Cause has ordained in lines of pure Stoicism. He tells Aumale,

> Good sir, believe that no particular torture
> Can force me from my glad obedience
> To anything the high and general Cause
> To match with his whole fabric hath ordain'd:
> And know ye all (though far from all your aims
> Yet worth them all, and all men's endless studies)
> That in this one thing, all the discipline
> Of manners and of manhood is contain'd:
> A man to join himself with th' Universe
> In his main sway, and make (in all things fit)
> One with that All, and go on round as it;
> Not plucking from the whole his wretched part,
> And into straits, or into nought revert,
> Wishing the complete Universe might be
> Subject to such a rag of it as he.[58]

Here is a man so completely immersed in Stoic ideology that he becomes its spokesman. And as Chapman interrupts his play to consider one Stoic doctrine after another, the drama develops as a series of philosophical exercises. The dramatic possibilities of the tragedy are eventually lost in moralizing that becomes more important than the actions that called it forth. This is not so much an indication that Chapman lost control of his material as it is a sign that when he was composing *The Revenge,* his interest in Clermont and men like him had led to the use of the dramatic form only as a means of introducing his Stoical men into the society of other characters. Furthermore, the student reading *The Revenge* soon realizes that Chapman's development as a tragic dramatist reached its climax in *Byron's Tragedy.* While the later tragedies contain scenes which have real dramatic impact, these scenes occur in isolated places, often without very much relation to context. Even in *The Revenge* the focus is directed no longer at tragedy in and for itself but at men whose idealism renders them unfit for life.

Stoical man that he is, Clermont remains altogether superior to Fortune. He expresses his complete indifference to her power when he goes to meet the King's men, knowing that they are waiting to seize him:

> Chance what can chance me, well or ill is equal
> In my acceptance, since I joy in neither,
> But go with sway of all the world together.
> In all successes Fortune and the day
> To me alike are; I am fix'd, be she
> Never so fickle; and will there repose,
> Far past the reach of any die she throws.[59]

The Guise re-echoes Clermont's sentiment, when, speaking to Henry, he characterizes his friend as one "to whom the day and fortune equal are."[60] We see in the portrait of Clermont that Chapman no longer considers the vicissitudes of Fortune to be of any consequence; Fortune has become completely unnecessary to the validity of his tragic concepts. In the previous *Bussy* play, as well as in the *Byron* plays, Chapman finally discarded Fortune in favor of Destiny; in *The Revenge of Bussy* he fails to entertain any respect whatsoever for Fortune, his first complete portrait of a Stoical man picturing one whose wisdom advises him at all times to acquiesce in his destiny. This acquiescence is emphasized by Clermont's stated belief that each man has his own niche in life, with which he should be content:

> I note how dangerous it is
> For any man to press beyond the place
> To which his birth, or means, or knowledge ties him.[61]

Clermont has learned early what both Bussy and Byron had learned too late—

> Fortune raises
> Huge heaps of outside in these mighty men,
> And gives them nothing in them.[62]

Thus far we have confined the discussion of Stoicism in *The Revenge of Bussy* to the influence of those tenets comprising the general or conventional level with which Chapman has already revealed his familiarity in both *Bussy* and the *Byron* dramas. In *The Revenge,* however, the very doctrines that affected the tragic direction of the earlier plays so little have assumed a different role, for they have now begun to control the development of both situation and character. Chapman uses the concept of Reason, for example, as an excuse for delaying Bussy's revenge while he explores the many facets of Clermont's individuality. Again, the dramatist, adhering to the dictates of Reason, at the same time denies the emotions, for he has created in Clermont a man whose insistence on calmness of mind and spirit enables him to ignore any temporary satisfaction the emotions may provide. Clermont's refusal to recognize any other world than that of the mind demonstrates clearly that too strict a devotion to even the commonplaces of Stoicism can rob a tragedy of the conflict essential to all drama. When Chapman combines the more serious aspects of Stoicism with the fundamentals of the philosophy, he clearly demonstrates the complete incompatibility existing between Stoicism and the theater in general, between Stoicism and tragedy in particular.

As we have noted earlier, out of the general concept of conduct grew the Stoic doctrine of willing things not as man might wish them, but as they are. In *Byron's Tragedy,* Chapman illustrated this Stoic tenet in Byron's efforts to overpass his proper station without respect for his King. In *The Revenge,* Chapman returns to this idea, exploring again the King's relation to his subjects. In the *Byron* plays, for example, as well as in *Bussy D'Ambois,* men conspire to depose a king. In the sequel to *Bussy,* however, no such conspiracy is evident. In Scene 1 of Act II, Baligny simply takes advantage of what the Guise later terms the King's "jealous ear" to tell Henry that

> The faction of the Guise . . .
> Grows ripe, and must be gather'd into hold.[63]

Baligny's treacherous remarks to Henry about the Guise and Clermont are based largely on the fact that these two men are fast friends—that is the extent of their fault. But as Chapman discusses the problem, he assigns Clermont and the Guise to one side, and Baligny and the jealous King, who finally has the Guise killed on a suspicion of treason, to the other. Actually, both sides are seeking to maintain the natural order, with the King as supreme ruler over his subjects. Clermont and the Guise, however, seek to maintain that order only because it preserves man in the security that proceeds from his acquiescence in the *status quo;* Henry and Baligny seek

to maintain it, not because they are good statesmen, like the King
in the *Byron* plays, but simply because that order sustains their
power.

Chapman has couched the argument in Stoic terms. Before Clermont has spoken a line, Epernon reports,

> He's now whispering in
> Some doctrine of stability and freedom,
> Contempt of outward greatness, and the guises
> That vulgar great ones make their pride and zeal,
> Being only servile trains, and sumptuous houses,
> High places, offices.[64]

Clermont's contempt for the outward show of offices, coupled
with other Stoic virtues, makes him incapable of Byron's sin of
aspiring too high. Baligny, on the side of the King who has been
led to fear that the Guise and Clermont seek to depose him, nevertheless plots their overthrow as the King's self-appointed spy. He
likens the King to the King of Kings, whom neither Reason nor
law nor conscience may criticize—the King is the supreme ruler.
Baligny's position is further emphasized when he disputes with
Clermont and the Guise over Brutus. The Guise sees no difference
between Clermont and Brutus except that Brutus was a "conspirator."[65] One is reminded at this point of Byron, a man who for a
time at least appealed to Chapman's Renaissance sympathies, for
Byron, too, was a conspirator. Having already told Henry that
"treachery for kings is truest loyalty,"[66] Baligny cannot understand
that being a conspirator should "impair" Brutus; for he regards
him not as one who aspired too high, but as one who "would be
the gods' just instrument"[67] when "Caesar began to tyrannize."[68]
But Baligny confuses the issue at several points. If any allusion to
Byron was intended, it lacks significance since Henry never be-
haved like a tyrant to Byron. If, on the other hand, Baligny intends

to defend Brutus' conspiracy against Caesar, his words still lack conviction, for such a defense is not in character with his earlier opinion that no man may justly question the King's "universal right."

In the first scene of Act III, Maillard and Chalon briefly weigh the ethical justification of their seizing Clermont when he arrives at Cambrai. They both agree that for one's King one must give up everything, since all true subjects should serve him "without disputing."[69] Thus far, Clermont has not expressed his own opinion of the extent of his duty to his King. But when Maillard approaches him at Cambrai, Clermont, after questioning his purpose, states that "acts that are done by kings are not ask'd why,"[70] a conclusion Byron also came to when he learned he must die. Clermont's conclusion, however, reveals him as a man who does not choose to struggle against things as they are, not because that is an easier course to follow but rather because he does not demand from life the kind of reward so necessary to men like Bussy and Byron.

It is the Countess of Cambrai who finally concludes the discussion. Learning that Clermont has fallen into the King's hands, the Countess comes to the crux of the relationship between king and subject. Since kings are compared to Gods, she believes they "should be like them";[71] when they punish "subjects' errors with their own," they abuse their power:

> So kings to subjects crying, "Do, do not this,"
> Must to them by their own examples' strength,
> The straightness of their acts, and equal compass,
> Give subjects power t' obey them in the like;
> Not shoot them forth with faulty aim and strength,
> And lay the fault in them for flying amiss.[72]

And knowing that Clermont could not be a traitor to his King, she characterizes him in all his Stoic honesty as one who

> was credulous;
> He would believe, since he would be believ'd;
> Your noblest natures are most credulous.
> Who gives no trust, all trust is apt to break;
> Hate like hell-mouth who think not what they speak.[73]

This discussion, appearing at intervals, keeps *The Revenge* from achieving the unity of the *Byron* plays, in which the subject-king controversy constitutes a major part of the so-called action. Though Chapman here relates the whole problem to Clermont, who is suspected of treason, Clermont does not actively participate in governmental affairs. Despite the fact that Cicero and Marcus Aurelius urged men to take an interest in government because participation in civic matters benefits both the citizen and the State, Chapman seems not to have shared this view as he developed the character of Clermont. The principled life of this Stoical man does not permit him to engage actively in the realm of public affairs, even though he moves within that world. The single theme that unifies the *Byron* plays now appears only as one of a great number of Clermont's interests, no one of which is strong enough in itself to give unity to the whole drama.

As one might expect, Clermont moves through life indulging in none of those emotional outbursts so typical of both Bussy and Byron. His lines are noteworthy for philosophic calm rather than for passionate fervor. Consequently, the world of *The Revenge* is a quiet world in which the mind remains untroubled by external events. Clermont devotes himself to the inner things, disregarding the externals which the Stoics believed prevented man from attaining peace of mind. That Chapman made this distinction deliberately, the text often demonstrates. Epernon, seeing Clermont hanging "upon the ear of Guise,"[74] remarks,

> He's now whispering in
> Some doctrine of stability and freedom,
> Contempt of *outward* greatness.[75]

Clermont himself quotes Epictetus to Renel to justify his own quiet
pursuit of the things of the mind:

> And for these idle outward things (says he) [Epictetus]
> Would'st thou lay on such cost, toil, spend thy spirits?
> And to be void of perturbation,
> For constancy, sleep when thou would'st have sleep,
> Wake when thou would'st wake, fear nought, vex for nought,
> No pains wilt thou bestow, no cost, no thought?[76]

And Clermont deliberately avoids an excess of emotion, as we note
in these essentially Stoic lines:

> Chance what can chance me, well or ill is equal
> In my acceptance, since I joy in neither,
> But go with sway of all the world together.[77]

He will exercise his self-control; he will be temperate, for "all is
one,"[78] "all must be borne."[79] Even when Clermont learns of the
Guise's murder, he refuses to yield to the tears that please, as the
Countess says,

> better
> Than all life's comforts, being the natural seed
> Of hearty sorrow,[80]

the tears that Epictetus condoned when they were shed "for com-
panie['s]"[81] sake. Clermont's control, however, has reached such a
state of perfection that he can plead,

> let me use
> Freely mine own mind in lamenting him.[82]

Parrott and Ball's statement that Clermont "will perform it [the revenge] . . . with neither haste nor passion"[83] is true generally of Clermont's every action, for he has trained himself to act with restraint at all times, so much so that his revenge of Bussy's murder appears of less consequence to him than his completely sincere devotion to his friend, the Guise.

No other of Chapman's tragedies explores so fully the friendship between two men as does *The Revenge*. Not only does the masculine nature of friendship stressed by the Stoics meet with the dramatist's full approval, but a corresponding disparagement of women, which the Stoics did not stress, also appears. The death of Clermont's friend even motivates his own suicide. Clermont does not lose his life when he avenges Bussy's death by killing Montsurry; but he decides to take it when he learns that the Guise has been murdered. This unusual twist to the usual denouement of the revenge-tragedy must have seemed as strange to the audience as it appears to the reader today. To die for one's friend was not without dramatic precedent, but to choose to follow a friend in death can be made intelligible only when we understand both the Stoic emphasis on friendship among men and the Stoic approval of suicide.

Chapman took several opportunities in *The Revenge* to remind his audience of the close bond existing between Clermont and the Guise. Early in Act I, Clermont is described as the Guise's "dear minion";[84] later we learn that they so "devour each other with" their "virtue's zeal" that nothing remains "for other friends." The Guise tells us,

> Clermont is my love;
> France never bred a nobler gentleman
> For all parts.[85]

Clermont himself in talking with Baligny praises the Guise in lavish terms, concluding,

Rich, poor of reason, wander; all pale looking,
And trembling but to think of their sure deaths,
Their lives so base are, and so rank their breaths.
Which I teach Guise to heighten, and make sweet
With life's dear odours, a good mind and name;
For which he only loves me, and deserves
My love and life, which through all deaths I vow:
Resolving this, whatever change can be,
Thou hast created, thou hast ruin'd me.[86]

When Clermont explains his conception of love to the Guise, the latter counsels,

Thy love being judgment then, and of the mind,
Marry thy worthiest mistress now being blind.[87]

But Clermont does not even consider marriage—

For when love kindles any knowing spirit,
It ends in virtue and effects divine,
And is in friendship chaste and masculine.[88]

This strong belief in the strong bond between two male friends receives its great test when Clermont learns of the Guise's murder. For him,

friendship is the cement of two minds,
As of one man the soul and body is,
Of which one cannot sever, but the other
Suffers a needful separation.[89]

Charlotte accepts Clermont's suicide, believing, "Loss of such a friend/ None should survive,"[90] and the Countess' words, "He liv'd but in the Guise,"[91] are a fitting epitaph to Clermont's devotion to friendship.

The masculine quality of this marriage of minds which Chapman presents with such strong personal conviction is heightened by a corresponding lack of respect for marriage between man and woman. Montsurry's disgust with Tamyra's persistent love for the dead Bussy leads him to make a comparison between "worthiest poets" and "worthiest women,"[92] denying women's lack of modesty in their "outparts." His comparison is touched with cynicism in that Montsurry takes more offense at women's ill deeds which lack "good show" than at their adultery itself. Tamyra blames the defects of marriage on the husbands who force their wives to "fit their disposures" without allowing them "their own affections." A cynical tone also pervades the conversation of Aumale and Maillard. The latter swears

> To touch no woman (to the coupling ends)
> Unless it be mine own wife, or my friend's.
> I may make bold with him.[93]

Aumale agrees:

> 'Tis safe and common.
> The more your friend dares trust, the more deceive him.[94]

This cynicism toward the sanctity of the marriage tie springing from people whose lives place them in marked juxtaposition to Clermont emphasizes his own ethical position. The Guise comments to him,

> How strangely thou art lov'd of both the sexes;
> Yet thou lov'st neither, but the good of both.[95]

Clermont's love of "the good of both" has resulted in a physical contact with women "like other lovers,"

> but, fruition past,
> I then love out of judgment.[96]

And it is this judgment associated with Reason that Clermont prefers. He will not accept, however, a marriage which recognizes love as judgment "and of the mind," as the Guise has suggested, since he believes there is no true love in marriage; he denies

> that any man doth love,
> Affecting wives, maid, widows, any women . . .
> So, when humanity rules men and women,
> 'Tis for society confin'd in reason.
> But what excites the bed's desire in blood,
> By no means justly can be constru'd love.[97]

This sharp demarcation between sexual satisfaction and the ultimate satisfaction in a masculine friendship founded on mental compatability has the full approval of the Stoics, Chapman's idealization of masculine friendship being nothing but a reflection of a similar emphasis among the Stoic philosophers. To a great extent, Chapman's adoption of the doctrine, for whatever reason, accounts for the fact that few women are to be found in the tragedies. Neither in the *Byron* plays nor in *The Revenge* do we encounter a woman of Tamyra's importance. And, while the women's roles are of greater importance in *The Revenge* than in either *Byron's Conspiracy* or *Byron's Tragedy*, they do not directly affect the dramatic action. All the important events occur in a masculine world in which ideas more often lead to an outpouring of words than to a development of any real conflict.

Clermont's fundamentally Stoic attitude towards his death is an example of Chapman's failure to portray death with dramatic interest and effectiveness. One need not know that Clermont is the Stoical man par excellence to realize that his death can be of little consequence to an audience, since he himself faces life with a characteristic "all is one" frame of mind. For no audience can be expected to take a greater interest in the death of the hero than he himself evinces. The first indication of Clermont's indifference to life comes when Renel taunts him with the thought that

> The people
> Will never know, unless in death thou try,
> That thou know'st how to bear adversity.[98]

Clermont's answer,

> I shall approve how vile I value fear
> Of death at all times,[99]

later serves as the measure of the Guise's Stoical development under Clermont's tutelage, for the pupil, lacking his master's equanimity, contemplates his own death with fear. The Guise does not find death natural; his reason cannot dominate his fear of it, and he yearns for Clermont's presence that he may again find strength to control his flesh's "softness."[100] But Clermont does not come, and the Guise is murdered, not in abject fear, yet without that contempt for death that Clermont at all times maintains. For Clermont's decision to die is a logical conclusion that enables him to face Death with quiet dignity:

> Since I could skill of man, I never liv'd
> To please men worldly, and shall I in death,
> Respect their pleasures, making such a jar
> Betwixt my death and life, when death should make
> The consort sweetest, th' end being proof and crown
> To all the skill and worth we truly own?[101]

His interpretation of death as nothing but a freeing of the soul from the confines of the body is in the best Stoic tradition:

> The garment or the cover of the mind
> The human soul is; of the soul, the spirit
> The proper robe is; of the spirit, the blood;
> And of the blood, the body is the shroud.[102]

In *The Revenge of Bussy D'Ambois,* Chapman has merged the Stoic disregard for death with suicide, which the Stoics fully condoned under certain circumstances. While the Stoic authors did not include the loss of a friend among those circumstances, Clermont's suicide does not appear ethically reprehensible by their standards, for, as Spencer writes, Clermont "did it, not because of any overwhelming disaster, but merely because his purpose in life was accomplished, and he had nothing left to live for."[103] It may be argued that Chapman was forced to conclude *The Revenge* with Clermont's suicide since Clermont had been permitted to survive Montsurry, the object of Bussy's revenge. The revenge-tragedy, which was to a certain extent Chapman's pattern, had not developed artistically to the point where the death of Montsurry could provide a satisfactory conclusion to the tragedy. The Jacobean audience would undoubtedly have felt cheated had Clermont survived the final curtain. But it was no such practical demand that dictated Clermont's suicide. We have already noted that Clermont's friendship for the Guise had not gone unnoticed by Baligny, Renel, or Monsieur. Clermont's own choice of masculine friendship in preference to marriage, coupled with the fact that Clermont regards the Guise as deserving of his "love and life," had made that friendship an essential factor in Clermont's decision to take his own life after the Guise's murder. The Countess' pointed statement that Clermont lived only in the Guise serves to substantiate this view. Mills' belief, then, "Since the friendship of Clermont and Guise has not been particularly stressed in the play, it looks as if Chapman rather calls in a reasonable motive to account for the death of a person whom for dramatic purposes he wishes to dispatch,"[104] seems hardly correct. The importance of that friendship to Clermont has been mentioned often enough to make it a crucial consideration, whether or not one deems the subject "particularly stressed." Mills' further statement, however, that "the loyal, philo-

sophical character of Clermont makes it a fitting motive"[105] must be
regarded as essentially sound, for that "philosophical character" to
which Mills refers springs directly from the doctrines of Stoicism
that not only placed great stress on friendship but also permitted
a man to commit suicide. Chapman's use of suicide for dramatic
purposes in *The Revenge* was a natural outgrowth of his earlier
emphasis upon the nobility of friendship. That it was not merely
a device that Chapman selected to resolve a single dramatic action
is clearly demonstrated in the later *Caesar and Pompey,* in which
Cato also commits suicide, though in his case it is not devotion to
friendship that affects his choice. Certainly nothing could indicate
more clearly the full extent to which Chapman had succumbed to
Stoic influences than his introduction in *The Revenge* of death
through suicide: and "In this Stoic fashion," as Spencer states,
"the Elizabethan emphasis on death was most fully expressed."[106]

Though it may seem, as Smith says, that *The Revenge* "merely
repeats . . . the commonplaces of Stoicism,"[107] it is, nevertheless,
a rich fulfillment of the promise of a sequel that Chapman had
made in the Epilogue of *Bussy D'Ambois.* Written when Chapman
was reading Epictetus and at the same time working on his major
translations, *The Revenge* clearly reveals that Chapman created in
the nonhistorical character of Clermont a man who invites comparison with both Bussy and Byron simply because as an ideal
Stoical man he is everything they are not. And one cannot help feeling that the Epilogue to *Bussy* is chiefly important because it was
added after the two *Byron* plays had been written and while Chapman was considering creating a character who might become a man
of principle more worthy of admiration than either Bussy or Byron.

But Chapman's preoccupation with Clermont unfortunately does
not carry with it any noteworthy development of his technique in
writing tragedy. For, although *The Revenge* does not betray the
obviously experimental quality of *Bussy,* neither does it indicate

that Chapman had benefited from having successfully written a dramatic epic as closely unified as the Byron story. As a result, *The Revenge* appears to be a tragedy in which Chapman's interest in Bussy's revenge represents little more than respect for the combination of audience and box office; yet, having committed himself early in the play to this popular subject, he is artist enough to conclude that particular action with Montsurry's death. This death, however, can in no sense be considered the climax of the entire play, for Clermont remains Chapman's dominating interest in *The Revenge*. In filling the intervening acts between Montsurry's death and the ending of the drama with more words than action, as was his custom, and in closely identifying all of Clermont's views with the tenets of Stoicism, Chapman failed to achieve a character as impressive as Byron, whose whole dramatic life exemplified the driving force of a single purpose. Clermont's lines in *The Revenge* in one way or another touch upon every aspect of the Stoic ethics, and the number of times *The Revenge* comes to a complete stop while Chapman explores this or that ethical implication is a clear demonstration of what must happen when the dramatist makes one character the mouthpiece of a whole system of ethics. Dramatic action cannot be made to support such large-scaled exposition; balance between word and deed becomes utterly impossible. In *The Revenge,* in particular, Chapman finally forces the audience to accept Clermont's death as tragic without making that acceptance even plausible. We listen carefully, but we do not always believe, since Chapman fails to make our belief necessary to his purpose.

For, in spite of the fact that Chapman has presented a picture of the almost perfect Stoical man, or perhaps because of it, his clearly delineated Stoic protagonist fails to stir us. We may admire Clermont's determination,

> To love nothing outward,
> Or not within our own powers to command;

And so being sure of everything we love,
Who cares to lose the rest? If any man
Would neither live nor die in his free choice,
But as he sees necessity will have it
(Which if he would resist, he strives in vain)
What can come near him, that he doth not [will,]
And if in worst events his will be done,
How can the best be better? All is one.[108]

But we must question the value of such determination when it occurs in dramatic tragedy: Clermont may shun all struggle, but without that struggle there can be no drama whatever. Clermont's Stoical conception of the will leads to his almost complete acquiescence in all of life's demands just as it fails to "generate an action."[109] Similarly, Clermont's suicide, although it is the logical conclusion to the ethical course of his life, tempts us to repeat Tamyra's judgment: "Too easy 'tis to die."[110] In particular, it is "too easy" in a tragic play, for tragedy grows from an action into which a character is forced by circumstances over which he can no longer maintain control. Clermont, however, chooses to commit suicide simply because life no longer appeals to him when the Guise is dead. With his choice there can be no argument, but that choice annuls rather than enhances whatever tragic impact the play might have otherwise attained. "The result is," as Smith remarks, "that when Clermont dies I am affected, not as with a tragedy, but as with a person's moving out of hearing, or with the stopping of a gramophone."[111]

In short, though *The Revenge* reveals on practically every page Chapman's complete familiarity with the Stoicism of both Epictetus and the neo-Stoics at both levels, it demonstrates at the same time that Stoicism must mean the negation of the tragic concept. Chapman's acceptance of the Stoic ethics caused him to create in Clermont a character far removed from the lives of most men, so far in fact that his deliberate death seems neither unexpected nor regrettable, but rather a fitting end for one whose ethical code prevented him from becoming a great tragic hero. In *The Revenge of Bussy,* Chapman has lost his objectivity to such an extent that Stoic doctrines now fully determine his purpose; the result is a drama that fails to produce an effective catharsis.

CHAPTER FOUR: THE TRAGEDY OF CHABOT ADMIRAL OF FRANCE

So his acts be just,
He cares for gain no[r] honour.

Act II, Scene 2, 11. 86-87.

THE DATING of *The Tragedy of Chabot Admiral of France* presents a problem that calls for re-examination. On the basis of known facts about Chapman's life, Professor Parrott's opinion that the play was written between 1611(?) and 1621-22 and Mrs. Solve's that it was composed between 1621 and 1624 represent two tenable theories; yet a consideration of the theme of this play in relation to the general intellectual and artistic development of Chapman leads the present writer to believe that *Chabot* in its original form dates from about 1612. Its kinship with *Caesar and Pompey* seems to point to this early date.

That Chapman wrote *The Tragedy of Chabot* before *The Tragedy of Caesar and Pompey* is, however, by no means certain. In his "Introduction" to the *Chabot*, contained in the 1910 edition of *Chapman's Tragedies*, Professor Parrott states, "It is clear that *Chabot* cannot have been written before 1611, and may have been written any time thereafter, before or after 1621."[1] This judgment is based on the fact that Chapman's source for this tragedy, Pasquier's *Les Recherches de la France*, "received its definitive form in 1611, in the twelfth chapter of the fifth book, entitled *Du procês extraordinaire fait, premierement à Messire Philippe Chabot Admiral de France, puis à Messire Guillaume Pouyet Chancelier.*"[2] But, as Parrott goes on to point out, the exact dating of this play is complicated by the fact that Chapman was not its sole author. The title page of the first edition of *Chabot* (1639) asserts that it was "written by *George Chapman,* and *James Shirley.*"[3] Consequently, "the approximate date will depend in some measure upon the view we take of the nature of Shirley's connection with this play. Did he collaborate with Chapman in its composition, or did he revise an old play by the elder poet?"[4] Inclining toward the latter conclusion, Professor Parrott then attempts to distinguish between the scenes which are pure Chapman and those which are new and by Shirley, at the same time indicating the scenes in which there is evidence of both hands. His decisions are substantiated to a certain extent by the present writer who has found little evidence of Chapman's thinking in the scenes that Parrott has stamped as pure Shirley, and passages that seem unmistakably to be Chapman's in those scenes which reflect both hands. Professor Parrott concludes,

Finally, I would suggest, though with no great positiveness, that Chapman wrote this play late in 1612 or early in 1613, when he was reduced to poverty by the death of his patron, Prince Henry; that he handed it over to the company of the Queen's Revels under the management of his friend, Nat. Field, and that it passed from them to the Princess Elizabeth's men, with whom this company united in 1613, and in whose possession it remained after they took the name of Her Majesties Servants in 1625. This was the company with which Shirley was identified; all his plays, with but one exception, *The Changes,* from his début until his departure for Ireland in 1636, were composed for them. And this is the company that performed *CHABOT.* What is more probable than the conjecture that shortly after Chapman's death, May 12, 1634, Shirley's attention was called to an old play by the famous poet still in their possession, and that he at once set to work to revise it for reproduction?[5]

Having thus tentatively established a composition date for this play

of joint authorship, Professor Parrott in his "Introduction" to
Caesar and Pompey then writes that this play "was composed about
the time of, probably a little later than, the *Revenge of Bussy,* i. e.
in 1612-13,"[6] thereby giving the first version of *Chabot* and *Caesar
and Pompey* the same date, 1612-13.

But in 1928, Mrs. Norma Dobie Solve, in her study, *Stuart
Politics in Chapman's "Tragedy of Chabot,"* feeling that *Chabot* reflects Chapman's interest in the English political scene, states, "It
is at this time, after the conviction of Bacon and before Somerset
had received a pardon, that is after March, 1621, and before De-
cember, 1624, that I believe Chapman wrote *The Tragedy of
Chabot, Admiral of France.*"[7] In his review[8] of Mrs. Solve's work,
Professor Parrott comments further on her dating of the play: "I
would suggest in passing an earlier date for the *terminus ad quem,*
i. e. the release of Somerset from prison in January 1622," but
he agrees in general with her thesis: "Mrs. Solve then may be said
to have proved her case, at least so far as proof in such matters
is at all possible."[9] There can be no doubt of the plausibility of
Mrs. Solve's contention, and on the basis of the evidence which she
has so logically presented, there is apparently little room for factual
disagreement.

Yet this date of 1621-22—1624 for the composition of *Chabot*
cannot be adopted without first considering several provocative
questions that its acceptance at once raises. In the first place, we
should then have to believe that, with the exception of the 1612-13
Caesar and Pompey, a period of almost ten years elapsed after *The
Revenge of Bussy* before Chapman wrote *Chabot,* a period during
which so far as can be ascertained he produced no dramatic work.
Nor is there any reason to believe that Chapman wrote either comedy or tragedy after the 1621-24 date.[10] But it is difficult to believe that this deduction represents the whole truth of the matter.
We have seen that the two *Bussy* plays and the two *Byron* plays all

deal with some aspect of French history so adapted as to enable Chapman to comment on the political scene at the same time that he develops his interest in the Stoical man. Inasmuch as *Chabot* likewise derives from French history embodied in a source very close in date to his preoccupation with Stoicism in the years 1611-12, so much in evidence again in the character of Chabot, it would seem strange indeed that Chapman should have let so many years go by before he returned to Pasquier for the skeleton of the story upon which to base the topical tragedy of *Chabot*. It is particularly strange in view of the fact that we have to believe that the *Caesar and Pompey,* a drama of classical times far removed from the contemporary scene, demanded Chapman's attention during the interim. On the other hand, it is perfectly true that in spite of its classical setting, the tragedy of *Caesar and Pompey* is closer in spirit and emphasis to *The Revenge of Bussy* than *Chabot,* and may very well have followed *The Revenge.* It is, nevertheless, difficult to believe that at a time when French history had such a firm hold on Chapman's interest, he should have turned after *The Revenge* to *Caesar and Pompey* and then waited for an incident in English history to reawaken that interest as a source for one last tragedy with a contemporary theme. The acceptance of such an explanation is particularly difficult when that theme is of far greater importance than that of any other play except the *Eastward Ho,* which Chapman wrote jointly with Johnson and Marston.

It still seems more likely that *Chabot* was originally a Chapman play dating from about 1612 and that Shirley later revised it. We realize, nevertheless, that such a view in no way answers the very valid objection that it was not until October 24, 1638, that *Chabot* "was entered in the Stationers' Registers" and that it was "published in 1639."[11] While this long delay seems to strengthen Mrs. Solve's thesis, yet the date of *ca.* 1612 seems closer to the development of Chapman's interest in Stoicism and the kind of play it fostered.

Perhaps because of its joint authorship, the tragedy of *Chabot* has never attained, even among critics, the attention it deserves, for it is by no means an inferior play. In several respects it is one of the best in the Chapman canon. True, it contains no such dashing figures as Bussy or Byron, but Chabot himself strikes a better balance between word and deed than Clermont, whose most interesting thoughts are often completely divorced from his concern with the revenge of Bussy. The focus on the problem of king versus subject remains just as sharp as in the *Byron* plays, since Chapman avoids the many bypaths of a Stoic-haunted mind which he was tempted to explore in *The Revenge of Bussy*. *Chabot* is a better play in that, without losing any of his idealism, the author has taken the problem out of a world that seems to exist too often only in the mind, and placed it in one of practical reality. Furthermore, this tragedy gains the plausibility of life itself from Shirley's adding new scenes and rewriting earlier ones. Shirley's emphasis on the roles of the Queen and Chabot's wife, for example, adds to *Chabot* a vital and eternal quality far removed from its source in French history. Nor have three centuries dimmed the appeal of a situation, so obviously attractive to Chapman, that must arise inevitably in the political world when a man like Chabot in high office refuses to sacrifice justice under pressure from higher authority.

On the slightest of plots Chapman has developed the character of Chabot, another Stoical figure who moves through life with simple dignity that is often both noble and humble. But, though Chabot is fashioned from Stoic influences, Chapman has succeeded in creating a "Senecal man" whose Stoicism impresses us just as much as Clermont's, without forever reminding us of his philosophical heritage. Whereas in *The Revenge of Bussy* we must watch Chapman put Clermont together from doctrines culled from Epictetus and his followers, whose mouthpiece he becomes, in *Chabot* there is little or no evidence of this almost mechanical process. Chabot has developed from the same origins as Clermont, but obviously he no longer follows the doctrines methodically as a formula for successful living and dying; Chabot has followed them for so long that his belief in an inviolate justice is the mark of a mature man, in whose life precept and action have become one.

But despite the fact that Chabot's well-integrated Stoicism reveals itself almost entirely in his martyrdom to the cause of justice, evidences of that integration from the whole body of Stoic doctrine are, nevertheless, occasionally apparent. The first scene of *Chabot,* like the first scene of the preceding tragedies, briefly sketches for the audience the general tenor of the ensuing drama. That the drama is again to be an ethical one is made clear in Allegre's third speech:

> great men are not safe
> In their own vice where good men by the hand
> Of kings are planted to survey their workings.[12]

Nor is the distinction made in these lines pertinent only to *Chabot,* for it will be remembered that in the "Prologus" to *Byron's Conspiracy,* Chapman had warned his audience to "see in his revolt how honour's flood/ Ebbs into air, when men are great, not good."[13] In the *Conspiracy,* the dramatist placed the stress on the "great" man; in *The Revenge of Bussy,* he places it on the virtuous wise man who scorns greatness but who remains unaware of the social responsibility imposed by goodness. In *Chabot,* he finally lays the emphasis on the "good" man:

> stand free and fast
> And judge him by no more than what you know
> Ingenuously and by the right laid line
> Of truth, he truly will all styles deserve
> Of wise, just, good; a man, both soul and nerve.[14]

Chapman's distinction between the "great" and the "good" man was the logical outcome, not only of his consistent search for the ethical rapport that must rightfully obtain between king and subject, but also of his wider reading among the Stoic philosophers, particularly Epictetus. In *Chabot,* Chapman finally decided upon the extent of the mutual obligation existing between the man who rules and the man who is ruled. But not until he wrote *Caesar and Pompey* did he resolve the differences between the man who would be great and the man who would be good as well.

If, as we believe, Chapman wrote *Chabot* about 1612, then he was working on this drama at approximately the same time that he was finding Epictetus' demarcation between the "great" and the "good" man a source of real provocation. Indeed, Chapman became so interested in the differences between these two types of men that he felt it necessary to devote a poem to each of them. He begins "A Great Man" (1612) as follows:

> A great and politicke man (which I oppose
> To good and wise) is neuer as he showes.[15]

Chapman also considers the possibility that the great man might conceivably be good, for in a marginal note later in the same poem, he writes, *"How a good great man should employ his greatnesse"* opposite these lines:

> Nor [the great man] can endure, as a most deare prospect,
> To looke into his own life, and reflect
> Reason vpon it, like a Sunne still shining,
> To giue it comfort, ripening, and refining.[16]

The short poem entitled "For Good Men" (1612) states by way of contrast Chapman's faith in the absolute integrity of the good man:

A good man want? will God so much deny
His lawes, his witnesses, his ministrie?
Which onely for examples he maintaines
Against th'vnlearnd, to proue, he is, and raignes:
And all things gouerns iustly: nor neglects
Things humane, but at euery part protects
A good man so, that if he liues or dies,
All things sort well with him?[17]

The Stoic quality of these lines is at once obvious; and, knowing that "A Great Man" is derived "From Hieronymus Wolfius' translation of Epictetus, *Enchiridion,* LXXI,"[18] and that "For Good Men is taken from Epictetus, *Discourses,* III, xxvi,"[19] we may make two important deductions. In the first place, Chapman's differentiation between these two men was by no means a casual one. But, more significantly, Chapman's deliberate emphasis early in *Chabot* upon the two kinds of men with a stated preference for the "good" man may be taken as an indication of the extent, not only of the ethical intent of the drama, but also of the Stoical character of that intent.

There are other evidences of Stoic backgrounds in this tragedy of *Chabot.* Asall's comment to Allegre, that theirs is "a bad age the while!"[20] springs from the latter's observation, very much in the manner of Monsieur in *Bussy D'Ambois,*[21] that the good man is subject to "not only/ That which in Nature hath excuse."[22] Here we find a recurrence of the idea that the weakness of man may in some measure be due to a corresponding weakness in Nature herself. The Chancellor uses Nature as an excuse to tempt Montmorency, the Lord High Constable, to regard lightly his recent reconciliation with Chabot and his promise to his King: "You must know, my lord, that even in nature/ A man is *animal politicum.*"[23] But Chapman throws aside both Allegre's suggestion that man reflects Nature's weakness and the Chancellor's excuse that man follows Nature's politics. When the play ends, Allegre's loyalty to Chabot has been rewarded by his becoming secretary to the King; on the other hand, the Chancellor's political aspirations have come to naught with his banishment to prison for life. Nature thus survives the doubts that have been cast upon her, emerging as man's rightful pattern for his behavior if he will but take time to understand her fully and place faith in her laws. No better example of this conclusion can be found than Chabot, whose final triumph over the Chancellor is the vindication of his own faith in Nature's principles of justice.

This reliance on the abiding quality of justice has its roots in Reason, a faculty that both Chabot and his King reverence. That Chapman's devotion to Reason as an infallible guide still endured is attested by these lines glorifying God's wisdom:

> the Almighty Wisdom, having given
> Each man within himself an apter light
> To guide his acts than any light without him
> (Creating nothing not in all things equal)
> It seems a fault in any that depend
> On others' knowledge, and exile their own.[24]

Chabot's adherence to Reason is so much a part of his daily life that, unlike Clermont, he finds it unnecessary to call attention to its influence with specific references. The King, however, whose prosecution of the Admiral alienates the sympathies of the audience, must on several occasions indicate that his actions are not the result of erratic impulses. When Chabot ably defends his refusal to sign the Constable's bill, the King remarks in an aside,

> Was ever such a justice in a subject
> Of so much office left to his own swinge
> That, left to law thus and his sovereign's wrath,

Could stand clear, spite of both? Let reason rule it,
Before it come at law: a man so rare
In one thing cannot in the rest be vulgar.[25]

After Chabot has departed, however, the King decides to give the
Chancellor the opportunity to sift the Admiral's "greatness" for
evidence of "other over-sights" above high "gross over-weening."
In this new frame of mind, the King tries to persuade Montmor-
ency to go against Chabot. When he refuses, the King cautions
Montmorency,

Take heed you banish not yourself; be wise,
And let not too much zeal devour your reason.[26]

The King continues to distort Reason to bolster his attack on
Chabot's honor, greeting the Chancellor's announcement that the
Admiral has been condemned with these words:

Is't not a wonder
That men's ambitions should so blind their reason
To affect shapes of honesty, and take pride
Rather in seeming than in being just?[27]

But the confident manner in which Chabot argues that he cannot
be pardoned for a crime of which he was never guilty gives the
King pause, and he rejects his previous distortion of Reason to
comment in another aside,

This confidence in Chabot turns my judgment:
This was too wild a way to make his merits
Stoop and acknowledge my superior bounties,
That it doth raise and fix 'em past my art
To shadow; all the shame and forfeit's mine.[28]

In the King's return to right Reason, Chapman has not only
achieved a renewed emphasis on the importance of Reason to jus-

tice, but has also succeeded in demonstrating the Stoical quality of
Chabot's mind, which from the start had refused to permit the
King's wounded vanity to swerve him from his own reasoned
course. Chabot had not been indulging in idle talk when he refused to follow Allegre's advice to retire from the world:

> I walk no desert, yet go arm'd with that
> That would give wildest beasts instincts to rescue
> Rather than offer any force to hurt me—
> My innocence, which is a conquering justice
> A[nd] wears a shield that both defends and fights.[29]

The Admiral's decision to accept with a Stoic calm whatever lies
ahead glows with that certainty existing only in him who has found
the sure way of life; and Allegre's comment, "One against all the
world!"[30] is an accurate description of the Stoical man whose reason
enables him to meet life without flinching.

Yet when Chapman created the man to whom Reason was so
vital a criterion for successful living, he did not find it necessary to
rob him entirely of his emotions. He had at last achieved a bal-
anced portrait of his ideal Stoical man. No longer was it a question
of inclining either toward such Renaissance individualists as Bussy
and Byron, whose emotions and impulses were the motivating
forces of their lives, or toward such an antithetical hero as Clermont, whose reason and deliberation governed his somewhat de-
tached existence. Aumale does ask in *The Revenge of Bussy,* to be
sure, how the ambushed Clermont fought off all his assailants with
a spirit that

> Turns flesh to air possess'd, and in a storm
> Tears men about the field like autumn leaves?[31]

Clermont's single relapse from his controlled way of life, however,
appears not so much as a characteristic action as a deviation which

for the moment really makes him Bussy's blood relative. In the character of Chabot, Chapman demonstrates that Stoicism need not enervate emotion. The evidence comes not from any single fray such as that in which Clermont fought, for Chabot's only weapon is his strictly disciplined mind; but from that mind there comes on several occasions a more impassioned defense of truth and justice, a more energetic expression of loyalty, than Bussy, Byron, or Clermont ever utter. It is almost as if Chapman were consciously qualifying Stoic doctrine by showing that emotions may be called into play when man champions a moral cause that threatens to destroy him, because emotion then becomes an ally of Reason. The Admiral's acceptance of life is no servile, contemptuous acquiescence, but a noble expression of his belief that virtuous wisdom must eventually triumph over all odds.[32]

Similarly, Chabot's acceptance of death reflects a greatness of spirit essentially Stoic, a nobility that both Bussy's and Byron's volubility and Clermont's almost studied recital of appropriate doctrines never attain on similar occasions. The Admiral does not weary us with set speeches. So carefully has Chapman integrated all the details of this portrait of Chabot that we expect and get in a few lines of simple description a reaction to death both fitting and effective: it invites rather than demands belief. His statement that "death is the life of good men"[33] is as Stoical as it is direct, and it is not ostentatious. When his innocence has been proved, his premonition of death—

> I never had a fear of the King's justice,
> And yet I know not what creeps o'er my heart,
> And leaves an ice beneath it—[34]

does not disturb us; the ordeal has simply been too much for his proud spirit. And later, when the Queen inquires, "Does he [Chabot] keep his bed?"[35] his father-in-law's reply reminds us at once of Bussy's propping himself on his sword,[36] of Byron's comparing himself to a captain in the saddle,[37] and of Clermont's likening himself to a ship's stopping at a distant port:[38]

> In that alone
> He shows a fortitude; he will move and walk,
> He says, while his own strength or others' can
> Support him, wishing he might stand and look
> His destiny in the face at the last summons,
> Not sluggishly exhale his soul in bed
> With indulgence, and nice flattery of his limbs.[39]

While this report lacks the poetic fire of these protagonists' last words as well as their self-sufficiency at death's approach,[40] this very deficiency gives it an appealing, human quality. For there can be no doubt that the death speeches of Bussy, Byron, and Clermont were all conceived with an eye to the poetic line which we read with appreciation but never honor with full belief.

The comparatively few lines that Chapman devotes to Chabot's death[41] only strengthen this feeling, for they are rather a summation of the play's thesis than an attempt by Chapman to make Chabot's death an example of Stoic indifference. The Admiral's request,

> let not the story
> Of Philip Chabot, read hereafter, draw
> A tear from any family,[42]

a Stoic plea for the control of any display of grief, is the only indication in this play of Chapman's interest in the Stoic's preparation to die.

None of the various Stoical doctrines thus far discussed, however, represents the fundamental problem of the tragedy: the proper relationship between king and subject. Chapman's concern with the concept of justice is one in which Cicero had evinced an interest. From Cicero, Chapman had learned that "all things just are proper; all things unjust, like all things immoral, are improper."[43] Seneca had also emphasized the independent quality of justice: "No man is just who is attracted by anything in this virtue other than the virtue itself."[44] Chapman followed this dictum in *Chabot,* where the Admiral refuses to permit any other consideration to interfere with his devotion to the principle of justice:

> His [the King's] judgment nor his favour I respect,
> So I preserve his justice.[45]

In fact so seriously does Chabot take the responsibilities of his office that it is reported

>   there's no needle
> In a sun-dial, plac'd upon his steel
> In such a tender posture that doth tremble,
> The timely dial being held amiss,
> And will shake ever till you hold it right,
> More tender than himself in anything
> That he concludes in justice for the state:
> For, as a fever held him, he will shake
> When he is signing any things of weight,
> Lest human frailty should misguide his justice.[46]

Having established the Admiral's reputation for justice, Chapman then introduces a Courtier, bearing a bill for Chabot's signature, a bill which the King has already signed. But Chabot refuses to sign the Constable's suit, it

>   being most unjust, and he pretending
> In all his actions justice, on the sudden
> After his so late vow not to violate it,
> Is strange and vile; and if the King himself
> Should own and urge it, I would stay and cross it;

> For 'tis within the free power of my office,
> And I should strain his kingdom if I pass'd it.[47]

Not until the cause of justice has thus been placed above any personal duty to his King do we learn the nature of the suit out of which the remainder of the play develops. Chapman then introduces the question of the legality of giving a French ship to Spain as recompense for a Spanish ship that a Frenchman had seized prior to the signing by both countries of the League of Nice in 1538. This point of law is not referred to again during the entire course of the play; it is used only as the point of departure from which Chapman develops the case of the just subject whom the King cannot intimidate with any suggestion of royal prerogative. The dramatist devotes the remaining four acts of *Chabot* to an ethical consideration of the ruler and the ruled, resolving it in terms of the Stoic individual whose reasonable conduct gives him certain inalienable rights, rights that even kings must respect.

The magnificent third scene of the second act presents most clearly the two points of view championed by the King and Chabot, respectively. The King asks Chabot to be less "severe" to his Constable, Montmorency, whom he favors. He tells the Admiral that the day may come when he, too, may wish to avail himself of a similar "argument," that his stand does not "square" with his "gentle nature," since it fires his blood and makes his "love of justice" appear as jealous "envy." The King even tries to make his own love for Chabot a reason for the latter's dropping his opposition to the suit and insinuates that he, rather than Chabot, should decide the justice of the matter. But the King's arguments do not touch Chabot. He cannot change Chabot's mind; the Admiral remains adamant, placing his belief in righteous justice above the King's love for him. He disregards what people say of him, wishing only to serve the King's cause with honor:

> Myself am nothing,
> Compar'd to what I seek; 'tis justice only,
> The fount and flood both of your strength and kingdom's.[48]

When the King asks, "And who shall judge that justice, you or I?"[49] Chabot replies,

> I, sir, in this case; your royal thoughts are fitly
> Exempt from every curious search of one,
> You have the general charge with care of all.[50]

But the Admiral acts with no sense of false pride—he counters, when the King terms his position "brave,"

> No, sir, 'tis plain and rude,
> But true and spotless.[51]

The King rejects Chabot's defense, however, and his hurt pride leads him to investigate the Admiral's career for evidence of "stain." Thus the struggle is continued, though there is never any doubt that the cause of justice will emerge victorious. In the first scene of Act III, "almost wholly the work of Shirley,"[52] the hand of Chapman is nevertheless apparent in the character of Chabot's father-in-law, who approaches the controversy between king and subject from a point of view slightly different from any so far encountered. In this scene we see the Queen demanding from Chabot's wife the respect due her position at the same time that she denounces Chabot. Before the Wife has had time to marshall her arguments, her father intervenes with words of practical advice that bear the stamp of both Chapman and Stoicism:

> I must confess
> I am a man out of this element,
> No courtier; yet I am a gentleman
> That dare speak honest truth to the Queen's ear
> (A duty every subject wo' not pay you),

And justify it to all the world. There's nothing
Doth more eclipse the honours of our soul
Than an ill-grounded and ill-followed passion.[53]

These Stoic words direct the Wife's thinking, and she, too, turns
upon the Queen to criticize the sovereign power that abuses the
rights of subjects:

When sovereign princes dare
Do injury to those that live beneath them,
They turn worth pity and their pray'rs, and 'tis
In the free power of those whom they oppress
To pardon 'em; each soul has a prerogative,
And privilege royal, that was sign'd by Heaven.[54]

Professor Parrott, commenting on the nature of Shirley's revision of *Chabot,* states, "Shirley would cut down the long epic
speeches, cut out as much as possible the sententious moralizing, fill
in with lively dialogue, introduce, or at least strengthen, the figures
of the Wife and the Queen to add a feminine interest to the play,
and in general make it over for the stage of his day."[55] This statement probably comes very near the truth. Yet the lines quoted above
definitely contain that "sententious moralizing" that Shirley evi-
dently found it impossible entirely to delete. Furthermore, since
this play continues a subject which had already demanded much of
Chapman's attention, it is likely that this and similar passages from
scenes on which Shirley worked continue to reveal the hand of
Chapman. It should also be remembered that the Wife's moralizing
in *Chabot* is not a peculiarity of this play alone. In Scene 3 of Act
IV of *The Revenge of Bussy D'Ambois,* the Countess also demonstrates that Chapman had already created a woman with a deep
interest in the ethics of government:

Is society
(To keep which only kings were first ordain'd)
Less broke in breaking faith 'twixt friend and friend,
Than 'twixt the king and subject? Let them fear.
Kings' precedents in license lack no danger.
Kings are compar'd to gods, and should be like them,
Full in all right, in nought superfluous,
Nor nothing straining past right for their right:
Reign justly and reign safely.[56]

The King's joy in the Court's condemnation of the Admiral's "boldness" that he may now "pardon" Chabot proves short-lived, since that decision has not affected Chabot's confidence in the rightness of his opposition to the King: "You cannot pardon me, sir."[57] And when the King learns that the condemnation was secured from the judges under duress from the Chancellor, he can only admit that his own search for justice has lacked Chabot's wisdom and integrity:

How false a heart corruption has! How base,
Without true worth, are all these earth-bred glories![58]

The King realizes at the time of Chabot's approaching death that he himself is responsible:

I see it fall;
For justice being the prop of every kingdom,
And mine broke, violating him that was
The knot and contract of it all in him.[59]

So Chapman brings to an end this contest of wills between subject and king that had already appealed to his imagination in each of the tragedies based upon French history. In the Stoic's insistence upon an "independent and virtuous justice" and in Chabot's mature and noble embodiment of the Stoic individuality, Chapman has developed an ideal figure who places the good of the State above private gain. For Chabot is neither a Bussy nor a Byron in his refusal to recognize any limitation to personal aspiration. Nor is he a Clermont, who can live by the highest principles but remains powerless to translate those principles into actions for the general good. More than any other of Chapman's heroes, Chabot represents the feeling of social obligation that was Marcus Aurelius' particular contribution to Stoic ethics. Chabot thinks in terms of others as well as of himself, becoming the only character thus far in the tragedies who achieves something of the social consciousness that Stoicism approved at least in theory. He demands justice not for his own glory but for the good of the kingdom. Both the torture of his servant, Allegre, to force an admission of guilt on Chabot's part and the threatened unlawful seizure of a fellow countryman's ship arouse in Chabot a feeling of outraged justice. At the same time, his zeal for justice does not rob him of his personal responsibilities to his King. His loyalty remains above suspicion in his defense of the King addressed to his father-in-law when the latter urges him to leave the Court, though he readily acknowledges the fact that they do not always agree:

> we have such a master of our King,
> In the imperial art, that no power flies
> Out of his favour, but his policy ties
> A criance to it, to contain it still.[60]

In *Chabot,* Chapman has at last resolved the proper relationship of the subject and the king strictly according to Stoical standards. His solution maintains the *status quo;* things remain as they are. But both the king and the subject have common obligations to the State which transcend all personal bonds. The king must not interfere with the subject's efforts to secure justice for all; at the same time the subject must continue his respect and loyalty to the Crown, no matter what personal friction is engendered by any course of action that the good of the State demands. The subject must retain his liberty within the framework of the law; and only in so far as this liberty neither weakens nor destroys the kingdom, may the ruler rightfully demand the subject's allegiance. But when the desire for personal advancement outstrips the demands of public duty, the Chancellor, like Byron, must face destruction:

> My ambition now is punish'd, and my pride
> Of state and greatness falling into nothing.[61]

Chapman demands that neither the king nor the subject aspire to "greatness"—only when both men are satisfied with Stoic "goodness" can they be compatible members of the same social structure.

The Stoic authors and Chapman's *The Tragedy of Chabot Admiral of France* often create the same impression: the ethics of Stoicism are best suited to mature, experienced men. As one reads the Stoic philosophers, one is impressed with the fact that the rules of conduct they advocated best fit men who are seeking to find security in a world crumbling with age. Theirs is a world that drives them to seek solace in their last years and to pass along their ideas and ideals to young men, that they may follow the path more easily. Stoicism is not a philosophy for energetic young men because its teachers are more interested in controlling youthful spirits than in using those spirits to revitalize their own thinking.

So in the tragedies of Chapman, Bussy and Byron are young men whose youth appealed to Chapman's Renaissance sympathies even when the author was no longer young. But by the time he came to create the portrait of the Stoical Clermont, he was approximately fifty-five years old. Whether or not he, like Seneca, was then taking heed and reckoning up his losses, the fact remains that Clermont has left his youth far behind him. Though Chapman portrays Clermont as Bussy's brother, they are no more of the same age than they

are of the same mind. Again, Chabot in his very wisdom and
judgment must impress one as no longer young. His rebellion is
not that of a Bussy or a Byron, but of a man more like Clermont, of
one whose fire springs not from a fearless energy but from a fearless mind, developed and grown strong in ethical actions. He is the
Stoic protagonist whose words and deeds have achieved a fine balance from adult living with all kinds of men. As a result, Chabot
demands the respect due men whose idealism is compounded of experience and wisdom. About such a man Chapman could ask in
all fairness,

> If he be virtuous, what is the reason
> That men affect him not?[62]

About such a man, he could answer with our full understanding:

> The Admiral is not flexible, nor won
> To move one scruple, when he comprehends
> The honest tract and justness of a cause.[63]

But in spite of the fact that in the tragedy of *Chabot* Chapman
has succeeded in portraying a Stoical man whose life we know more
intimately than that of Bussy, Byron, or Clermont, he has, nevertheless, failed to write a tragedy that produces in the reader any semblance of Aristotelian catharsis. We find ourselves championing
Chabot's cause against the King, but the King's actions call forth
little of that deep indignation which would make the Admiral's
death seem a miscarriage of justice. Chabot's desire to live has been
destroyed by an "unkind"[64] King who simply illustrates the fact
that

> 'Tis dangerous to play too wild a descant
> On numerous virtue, though it become princes
> To assure their adventures made in everything.[65]

Yet, just as Clermont had nothing left to live for with Bussy avenged and the Guise murdered, so Chabot's wife, his father-in-law, and his King all fail to provide an adequate excuse for his clinging to life after his vindication. We therefore accept his death as we accept Clermont's with a feeling of relief that the troubles of this admirable Stoic are forever finished; we are not even tempted to shed the tear against which Chabot warns his "hereafter"[66] reader. These men, because they make death seem too easy, arouse in an audience no more regret than they themselves experience in their passing. The Stoic ethics has taught them how to accept life, but it has also robbed their deaths of tragic significance.

In *Chabot,* Chapman successfully fuses the conventional literary patterns of Renaissance Stoicism and some of the more serious aspects of the philosophy—the drama that ensues frequently reflects the extent to which the playwright has adoped Stoic doctrine as a way of life. But it also demonstrates clearly that when Chapman permitted the philosophy of Stoicism to dictate the conditions that make life acceptable, he achieved only the semblance of tragedy. The death of a Stoic protagonist simply affirms a devotion to ethical motives in which tragic meaning is never present.

CHAPTER FIVE: THE TRAGEDY OF CAESAR AND POMPEY

> Only a just man is a free man
>> From the title page, *The Tragedy of Caesar and Pompey.*

IF CHAPMAN wrote *The Tragedy of Caesar and Pompey* in 1612-13[1] after he had written *Chabot,* it was his last play. Turning from contemporary French history to that of ancient Rome, to an era in which the Stoic philosophy had had full development, Chapman was able to give free rein to his interest in the Stoical man. And as he wrote of Caesar, Pompey, and Cato, he added to at least one of these portraits details which we must believe represent his deep and abiding personal convictions. Chapman's mind was clearly more at home in the world of Rome than in sixteenth-century France.

"The Argument" prefixed to the first edition of the play (1631)[2] indicates not only the content and general plan of this tragedy, but also the differences among the three leading characters whom Chapman intended to exploit:

> Pompey and Caesar bring their armies so near Rome, that the Senate except against them. Caesar unduly and ambitiously commanding his forces; Pompey more for fear of Caesar's violence to the State, than moved with any affectation of his own greatness. Their opposite pleadings, out of which admirable narrations are made; which not yet conducing to their ends, war ends them. In which at first Caesar is forced to fly, whom Pompey not pursuing with such wings as fitted a speeding conqueror, his victory was prevented, and he unhappily

dishonoured. Whose ill fortune his most loving and learned wife Cornelia travailed after, with pains solemn and careful enough; whom the two Lentuli and others attended, till she miserably found him, and saw him monstrously murthered.

Both the Consuls and Cato are slaughtered with their own invincible hands, and Caesar (in spite of all his fortune) without his victory victor.[3]

When the author refers to "Caesar unduly and ambitiously commanding his forces," we are reminded of Byron, whose life was also devoted to an ambitious command of his men as a means to personal advancement. Chapman next introduces Pompey, moved "more for fear of Caesar's violence to the State, than . . . with any affectation of his own greatness," who reminds us again of Byron, to whom also greatness was more important than goodness. Pompey is like Chabot, too, in placing the welfare of the kingdom on a par with his own goodness. Finally, Chapman mentions "both the Consuls and Cato [who] are slaughtered with their own invincible hands, and Caesar (in spite of all his fortune) without his victory victor." This reference to suicide recalls Clermont, while Caesar's being victor without victory is reminiscent of the empty satisfaction of the King in *Chabot*, whose own unkindness caused the untimely death of the Admiral, his most loyal subject.

Chapman does not always make plain the purpose and direction of this tragedy. Confronted by Caesar, the kind of historical hero whose aspirations he had already condemned in the *Byron* plays, and by two Stoical protagonists, Pompey and Cato—three figures whose personal histories were closely interrelated and recorded in Plutarch[4]—Chapman seems to have selected for his title the names of the two men best known, despite the fact that Cato eventually claimed the preponderant share of his interest. On Cato, Chapman finally focuses his attention, but when in the course of the action the author attempted to divide his attention among these three characters, he was unable to present them with equal emphasis. The play, therefore, lacks unity.

It is striking that Cato's name does not appear in the title of the play, for it was Chapman's custom to name his tragedies for the central figure. Even though Clermont's name does not appear in the title of *The Revenge of Bussy D'Ambois,* the protagonist at least bears the D'Ambois name. In his last tragedy, however, Cato assumes far greater importance that Caesar, at times even more than Pompey, yet the title does not name him. Neither Caesar nor Pompey, however, represents fully Chapman's persistent interest in Stoicism as a way of life.

Chapman's Caesar is almost as deficient in Stoical qualities as Byron; yet, because of that very fact Caesar becomes as distinct a character as Pompey, whose Stoic development makes his death more memorable than his life. But despite his lack of sympathy for Caesar, Chapman has not distorted the facts of history to make him less a man than he actually was.

Developing the portrait of Caesar suggested in "The Argument," Cato tells us in the opening lines of the play that both Caesar and Pompey

> With their contention all the clouds assemble
> That threaten tempests to our peace and empire,
> Which we shall shortly see pour down in blood,
> Civil and natural wild and barbarous turning.[5]

It soon appears that Pompey and his army have been permitted to come near the City because Rome fears tyrannous Caesar, while Caesar in turn fears that Pompey has designs upon the Empire. Just as in the earlier tragedies Chapman had condemned duplicity and deceit as characteristic of hangers-on at Court, so here in lines reminiscent of *Sejanus,*[6] he attacks the "flock of puttocks" who attend Caesar:

> where Caesar goes there thrust up head
> Impostors, flatterers, favourites, and bawds,
> Buffoons, intelligencers, select wits,
> Close murtherers, mountebanks, and decay'd thieves,
> To gain their baneful lives' reliefs from him.[7]

But despite this scorn of Caesar, Chapman puts into Caesar's mouth a justification of his conduct. In a full meeting of the Senate at the Forum, Caesar defends himself in a Byronlike manner. He asks the assembly,

> Why . . . may it be esteem'd
> Self-praise in me to prove myself a chief,
> Both in my love of her [his country] and in desert
> Of her like love in me?[8]

Like Byron, too, Caesar boasts of his reputation and ability as a warrior, hoping that this

> service,
> . . . may interest me in her love,
> Public, and general enough, to acquit me
> Of any self-love, past her common good.[9]

When, however, Cato's relentless opposition to bringing into Rome either Pompey's or Caesar's armies to control any possible resurgence "of Catiline's abhorr'd conspiracy"[10] leads Caesar to order Cato's overthrow and his imprisonment, Pompey reminds Caesar that Cato's fear of their aspirations once their armies enter Rome may be well founded:

> For who knows
> That, of us both, the best friend to his country
> And freest from his own particular ends
> (Being in his power), would not assume the Empire,

And having it, could rule the State so well
As now 'tis govern'd for the common good?[11]

Chapman's continued preoccupation in *Caesar and Pompey* with
a ruler's threatened disruption of the social order reveals the dramatists' deep concern with the problems of government. And although the Stoical Cato is more like Clermont than any other of
Chapman's tragical heroes, yet Cato's insistence that the subject be
free to oppose the ruler in a just cause is closer to the character of
Chabot than to that of Clermont.

But it is not only Caesar's abuse of power that marks him as the
type of man Chapman had long since ceased to admire. Like Bussy,
whose reliance on Fortune Chapman had earlier found wanting in
tragical significance, Caesar is one of Fortune's sons. In his denial
that Fortune has ever had any part in his success, Pompey counters
that "some have said she was the page of Caesar."[12] Later when
Acilius accuses Fortune of being at fault in Pompey's defeat of
Caesar on the battlefield, Caesar refuses to condemn her, choosing
rather to make the fault his own: "It was not Fortune's fault, but
mine, Acilius."[13] Caesar's faith in Fortune is also shared by Antony,
who expects Fortune to change his emperor's luck. When Vibius
returns to Pompey with Caesar's offer of peace, Antony expresses
the belief that

> This prepares
> A good induction to the change of Fortune
> In this day's issue, if the pride it kindles
> In Pompey's veins makes him deny a peace
> So gently offer'd; for her alter'd hand
> Works never surer from her ill to good
> On his side she hath hurt, and on the other
> With other changes, than when means are us'd
> To keep her constant, yet retire refus'd.[14]

Comparable to Caesar's belief that Fortune directs his future is his Byronlike trust in the ability of the soothsayer to reveal that future. Just as Bussy's appeal to the supernatural powers and Byron's visit to the Astrologer mark them both as men who find it difficult to acquiesce in the decrees of Fate, so Caesar's appeal to the soothsayer indicates the wide gulf that exists between him and such Stoical men as Clermont, Chabot, and Cato.[15] Imperial Caesar rules the world but cannot rule himself; the three superior Stoical men rule themselves and the world does not trouble them.

But in spite of Chapman's expressions of distrust in Caesar's greatness, the playwright saw some good in Caesar, who was not willing ruthlessly to sacrifice his country to his own ends. After Pompey has once defeated him, Caesar appears alone on the stage. Though his fortunes are at a low ebb, he cannot believe that Fate has destined him for such absolute ignominy:

> I, that have ransack'd all the world for worth
> To form in man the image of the gods,
> Must like them have the power to check the worst
> Of all things that under their celestial empire,
> Stoop it, and burst it, or break through it all
> With use and safety.[16]

He then continues in lines that embody the very essence of the Stoic view of Nature—the purpose for which each man was framed:

> till the crown be set
> On all my actions, that the hand of Nature
> In all her worst works aiming at an end,
> May in a master-piece of hers be serv'd
> With tops and state fit for his virtuous crown.[17]

And Chapman gives Caesar the opportunity to refurbish the reputation that Pompey and Cato had damaged before the Senate. We find Caesar imploring the gods that he

May wipe the hateful and unworthy stain
Of tyrant from . . . [his] temples, and exchange it
For fautor of . . . [his] country.[18]

Of these lines, Professor Parrott writes, "Chapman breaks free from his sources . . . hinting, at least, at the true character of Caesar as it has been drawn by later historians, the man who made himself master of his country to save her from impending ruin and to re-establish her power on a more permanent foundation."[19] Moreover, in welcoming Brutus, Caesar proudly states that he himself has fought for the love of his country. Though he boasts before the Senate that he has personally slain in battle "twice fifteen hundred thousand" of his "dreadful enemies" and "a thousand thousand of them put to sword,"[20] Caesar nevertheless honors Roman blood[21] and worries about Cato's death lest he, Caesar, be branded as the murderer of one who also chose to fight for his country.[22] He can even criticize Brutus for censuring Cato's suicide since Cato "knew as well what fitted man, as all men."[23]

The reader, then, who relies on the Argument for Chapman's rounded opinion of Caesar entertains a distorted idea of Chapman's evaluation of him, for the description, "unduly and ambitiously commanding his forces," by no means tells the whole story. With Caesar's ambitions, with his willingness to be one of Fortune's darlings, Chapman was certainly not in sympathy. But he was wise enough to realize that Caesar was great despite his defects as a Stoic; he even seems to suggest that in Caesar, greatness and goodness are not as widely separated as he had demonstrated them to be in Byron. In Caesar, Chapman has portrayed the only man in all the tragedies who achieves heroic stature despite his almost complete independence of Stoic ethics.

Chapman's seeming uncertainty about the development of Pompey's character as the writing of *Caesar and Pompey* progressed is reflected in the fact that Pompey is not always as distinct a figure as Caesar. Yet it is obvious early in the play that Chapman has more sympathy for him than for Caesar. Even though Cato implies in his opening lines that both Caesar and Pompey are enemies of the State in that they threaten the peace of the Empire,[24] he expresses approval of Pompey before the Senate. And throughout the play Cato is more a *raisonneur* than any other character in the tragedies. When Caesar argues that Pompey's army need not enter Rome, Cato agrees, though he is certain that Pompey "affects not the Empire," "loves his country"; and he can disprove "the close aspersion/ Of his ambition."[25] Since Cato has referred earlier to "tyrannous Caesar," his approval of Pompey prepares the audience for a rapport between the two men somewhat like the understanding that existed between Clermont and the Guise, though, as we shall see, the two Romans are much less intimate friends.

As a friend of the Stoical Cato, Pompey naturally evinces a fine contempt for several of Caesar's non-Stoical traits. Having noted Caesar's reliance on the favors of Fortune, Pompey denies that he is in any way indebted to her:

> Yet her for me I both disclaim and scorn,
> And where all fortune is renounc'd, no reason
> Will think one man transferr'd with affectation
> Of all Rome's empire, for he must have fortune,
> That goes beyond a man.[26]

Stoic disapproval of the figure who would be more than a man may also be seen in the nature of Pompey's allegiance to the Emperor. In his debate with Caesar in the Forum, Pompey argues for that freedom of the subject to which Chabot's life was dedicated: the good citizen must place his duty to the State above that to an individual ruler:

> Nor will I see my country's hopes abus'd
> In any man commanding in her Empire,
> If my more trial of him makes me see more
> Into his intricacies, and my freedom
> Hath spirit to speak more than observers servile.[27]

While Pompey's decision to continue his campaign against Caesar—"Now to Pharsalia"[28]—is Stoic in its fearless resolution, it nevertheless contains an element foreign to Stoicism:

> And, therefore, what event soever sort,
> As I no praise will look for, but the good
> Freely bestow on all (if good succeed)
> So if adverse fate fall, I wish no blame,
> But th' ill befall'n me made my fortune's shame,
> Not mine, nor my fault.[29]

That Pompey should plan to be self-effacing in victory reveals adherence to the essentials of Stoic ethics; that he should, however, refuse to accept blame for possible defeat bespeaks a thoroughly non-Stoical attitude. For the true Stoic, like Clermont, to whom "all is one," should be as willing to accept defeat as victory, since his responsibility remains the same whatever the outcome. Brutus' question at this point is far more Stoical in substance than Pompey's statement which prompts it:

> Who more thirsts
> The conquest than resolves to bear the foil?[30]

Pompey realizes the significance of Brutus' query, but he insists that he not be blamed if he is defeated:

> Said Brutus-like! Give several witness all,
> That you acquit me whatsoever fall.[31]

Then Pompey drops from conversation while his friends discuss their leader's request. In a line reminiscent of Achilles' declaration in *The Odysseys* that *"none borne past others' Fates can pass his own,"*[32] the 2nd Consul states that "particular men particular fates must bear."[33] The King of Thessaly reminds the group that "he only conquers whose mind still is one,"[34] while the King of Iberia adds, "Who on himself sole stands, stands solely fast."[35] The King of Cicilia then counters with the practical consideration, "Who cares for up or down, when all's but thought?"[36] But Gabinius believes, "To 'hings' events doth no man's power extend."[37] And Demetrius contributes a remark that places the matter in the keeping of the gods: "Since gods rule all, who anything would mend?"[38] Then and then only does Pompey reenter the conversation: "Ye sweetly ease my charge, yourselves unburthening."[39] But the Stoic rationalizing with which Chapman seeks to minimize Pompey's responsibility in case of his defeat is not satisfactory. One has the feeling that the lines spoken by Pompey's staff were somehow meant to bring Pompey wholly within the bounds of Stoic doctrine, to make him and him alone responsible for the ensuing action. Consequently, the fact that Pompey's mind is eased only by the various sentiments the others express seems a defect in the dramatist's art, for Chapman extends to Pompey the possibility of immediately achieving full Stoic proportions, only to deny him for the present the realization of the opportunity.

Chapman later[40] pictures a Pompey in sharp contrast to that of the warrior determined to march toward Pharsalia, a Pompey who has lost his earlier Stoic resolution. He now reflects the confusion of his own forces, wondering why his men rush about "in panic terrors" without cause. He concludes:

> And what is this but even the gods deterring
> My judgment from enforcing fight this morn?[41]

He has even become the victim of superstition; the omens, he believes, are against him. It is not, however, Brutus's urging him not to forsake his "own wise counsel" that prevents Pompey from post-poning his battle with Caesar; it is his own fear of what people will say about him that troubles him:

> I cannot, sir, abide men's open mouths,
> Nor be ill spoken of . . .
> I bear the touch of fear for all their safeties,
> Or for mine own![42]

Vibius advises Pompey not to war against his own "Genius," but in an answer that may be accounted for only by his distraught state, Pompey in one breath threatens violence to anyone who urges him to bear the "scoffs and imputations" of those who talk about him and, in the next, orders his forces to battle. Pompey's whole man-ner indicates that the mantle of Stoicism has for the moment, at least, dropped from him, for the Stoic preached indifference to everything except the dictates of his own mind. Obviously, Chap-man's failure to maintain control of his material causes Pompey now to appear inconsistent with the character that he has thus far developed. Kern and Professor Parrott, long ago noting this very discrepancy, offered the following explanation:

> There [Scene 1 of Act III] the Pompey of Chapman's inven-tion, the calm, self-controlled Stoic, decides quietly and cheer-fully to hazard the decisive battle with Caesar. Here [Scene 1 of Act IV] we have the Pompey of Plutarch, driven against his will by the taunts of his followers to risk a contest, of whose successful issue he has little hope, in order to free himself of the charge of cowardice.[43]

The extent to which Chapman's earliest preoccupation with Stoicism had developed becomes apparent in his giving Pompey (Act III, Scene 1) a more Stoical character than that found in Plutarch, one of his Stoic teachers. The reversion of Chapman to

Plutarch's account in a short scene of only sixty-six lines is a puzzling lapse, for certainly the dramatist must have fully realized that the two faces of the portrait present contrasting views of the same character. This incongruity cannot be attributed to hasty composition or lack of time for revision, since a long interval seems to have elapsed between the date of composition and the date of publication. Nor does it seem probable that Chapman intended to introduce at this point in the tragedy a flaw in Pompey's Stoicism, there being on this one occasion only a clear-cut deviation from the ethics of the ideal Stoical man. Moreover, Pompey is no half Stoic. The final picture is not that of a man like the Guise, who never achieves full Stoic manhood, but of one whose Stoic faith develops from the experience of living, a faith that Pompey eventually finds equal to the demands of life. The reader must, therefore, regard this inconsistency in Pompey's character as a serious flaw in Chapman's art.

In the third scene of Act IV, Pompey regains some of his Stoical composure in the face of Caesar's victory. He can see now that he has been ruled more by the will of others than by his own—that he has acted against his better judgment. He can also see that "human confidence" may be a fault when that confidence is not justified. But he still refuses fully to assume the responsibility for this fault: his men "spotted" him with fear; he enjoyed too great a "love of glory." And Pompey remains non-Stoical, too, in his inability to accept the ways of gods to men:

> O, the strange carriage of their acts, by which
> Men order theirs and their devotions in them,
> Much rather striving to entangle men
> In pathless error than with regular right
> Confirm their reason's and their piety's light.[44]

Nor is Pompey's concern for his reputation worthy the self-sufficient Stoic who cares only for his opinion of himself:

> Whatever my untouch'd command of millions
> Through all my eight and fifty years hath won,
> This one day, in the world's esteem, hath lost.[45]

But as his outburst of self-pity passes, Pompey finds his solace in genuine Stoic doctrine. He admits to Demetrius and to himself that he allowed the battle with Caesar to excite him too much:

> I confess
> That till th' affair was past my passions flam'd;
> But now 'tis helpless, and no cause in me,
> Rest in these embers my unmoved soul
> With any outward change, this distich minding;
> "No man should more allow his own loss woes,
> (Being past his fault) than any stranger does."[46]

He has learned that

> every true soul should be here so sever'd
> From love of such men as here drown their souls
> As all the world does, Cato sole [excepted].[47]

So he and Demetrius disguise themselves, that their "habits" and their "fortunes" may appear as one—

> nor desire to be
> (Do Fortune to exceed it what she can)
> A Pompey, or a Caesar, but a man.[48]

Although certain elements of this scene are not Stoical in character, yet it is apparent that Pompey is here nearer in spirit to the Pompey of Act III than to that of Act IV. The explanation again lies in Chapman's departure from his source. As Professor Parrott writes, "For the most part . . . the scene is Chapman's invention, and the stoical temper exhibited by his Pompey in defeat is in strong contrast to the lethargy of despair described by Plutarch."[49]

We must, therefore, look upon Pompey as unique among Chapman's Stoical men, for the imperfections of the character as conceived by Chapman make of Pompey a more tragical figure than Cato. In Chapman's tragedies as a whole, the humanity of the author rarely penetrates the curtain of Stoicism through which he views his greatest protagonists, the men whom he deems "good." Yet, though Chapman did not produce in Pompey a finished Stoic, he did create a man whose humanity, whose human weakness, reveal him as a figure of true tragic significance simply because we can for once identify ourselves with that humanity, that weakness. It is ironic that Chapman's failure should have produced the only portrait of a Stoical man that our human understanding can readily accept. Forgetting for a brief time that *Caesar and Pompey* is a tragedy set in classical times, we share Pompey's feeling of despair of ever finding a habitable world, as we seldom share in the concerns of Clermont, Chabot, and Cato.

The final scene, in which Pompey comes home to his wife, Cornelia, more genuinely tragic than other death scenes of Chapman's Stoic men, produces an emotional effect that is in large measure due to the importance of Cornelia's role. Cornelia is the only feminine Stoic in all the tragedies; as such, she is a thoroughly suitable partner for her husband, Pompey.[50] And, as we have already twice noted, "Here, again, Chapman departs from his source to exalt the Stoic fortitude of his characters."[51]

Chapman does not permit the disguised Pompey and Demetrius to disclose themselves at once to Cornelia. Before they do so, we hear a conversation in which the Stoic qualities of Cornelia and Pompey are firmly established. On the one hand, we have Cornelia, who, knowing that Pompey is "truly good" and denying that she "must have her husband great," wins from the 1st Lentulus the praise that "she's a philosophress." Good Stoic that she is, it does not matter to her that her husband has fallen; she can submit her-

self cheerfully to him "if he submit himself cheerfully to his fortune."[52] When Pompey immediately retorts, " 'Tis the greatest
greatness in the world you under/take,"[53] Cornelia replies that she
"would be so great, if he were."[54] Thereupon Pompey reveals himself, after asking Cornelia to "make good" her greatness.

On the other hand, we have Pompey, now grown completely
strong in his Stoic beliefs. He has little to say while Demetrius with
his skillful interruptions prompts Cornelia to declarations that
show that a "learned"[55] woman may also qualify as a Stoic. But
after his disguise has been cast aside, it is Demetrius' turn to be
quiet while Cornelia and Pompey finally resolve in the last min-
utes of Pompey's life the question of greatness and goodness, an
ethical problem in which Chapman had become almost as interested as in the relationship of subject and king.

Pompey begins by expressing surprise that his wife remains as
"good" as when she was "greatest."[56] From his Stoic wife Pompey
has at last learned the nature and importance of goodness, the
quality which had made such a strong appeal to Epictetus:

> I now am good, for good men still have least,
> That 'twixt themselves and God might rise their rest.[57]

And when Cornelia tells him that he has never been " 'great' till
now," Pompey indicates just how close the relationship between
goodness and greatness must be:

> O, my Cornelia, let us still be good,
> And we shall still be great.[58]

Just as the Stoics came to believe that if a man would be great, he
must ignore outward things,[59] so Pompey now realizes,

> Griefs for wants outward are without our cure,
> Greatness, not of itself, is never sure.[60]

Cornelia's joy in finding Pompey "thus fix'd" also encourages him to admit,

> 'Tis enough for me
> That Pompey knows it. I will stand no more
> On others' legs, nor build one joy without me.
> If ever I be worth a house again
> I'll build all inward; not a light shall ope
> The common outway.[61]

Pompey's determination to emphasize inner things hereafter springs from his realization that a life devoted to worldly greatness is a denial of Reason:

> No ornament, no door will I use there,
> But raise all plain and rudely, like a rampier
> Against the false society of men
> That still batters
> All reason piecemeal, and, for earthy greatness,
> All heavenly comforts rarefies to air.[62]

He will, therefore, in a spirit of *contemptus mundi* turn his back on the world, for, in so doing, Reason may then let in a purer light:

> When therefore our diseas'd affections,
> Harmful to human freedom, and, storm-like,
> Inferring darkness to th' infected mind,
> Oppress our comforts, 'tis but letting in
> The light of reason, and a purer spirit
> Take in another way.[63]

In the figure of Pompey Chapman gives us his only protagonist whose Stoical character was not already fully developed at the opening of the tragic action. We are permitted to watch him grow in his Stoicism; we even see in an artistic lapse a crack in Chapman's

Stoical armor. But the fact that we are permitted to watch Pompey forge from his defeat a conception of the properly good life accounts for the tragic significance of his portrait. We share equally in his despair and his eventual victory. As a result, we experience that emotional catharsis always essential to an authentic tragic experience. For the first time in a Chapman tragedy, we regret the death of a Stoical man, for Pompey's murder must seem a miscarriage of justice; for the first time, we experience a *positive* reaction to a Stoic's death. This death is no longer the negation of the tragic principle. Pompey is not ready to die; he has come to recognize the essential truths of every man's existence and has only now begun to live according to those truths. But Pompey must meet the fate that history had long ago determined, and the murderers lead him off after he has blessed his children and expressed the same hope for them that King Henry had expressed for the young Dauphin in *Byron's Tragedy*:[64]

> Even that high hand that hurl'd me down thus low,
> Keep you from rising high![65]

Pompey finally *becomes* a Stoic, but Cato *is* one. Cato's every action, like Chabot's, is an expression of Stoical principles.[66] Swinburne's statement, "The genius of the author comes in and goes out with Cato,"[67] at first seems hardly correct since Chapman has devoted only two scenes to a detailed analysis of Cato's mind. Certainly Cato is an important figure throughout the play, but it is the contrast that Chapman has drawn between Caesar and Pompey and between them and him that draws our attention to Cato. For the dramatist emphasizes not only the difference between Caesar and Pompey but also the difference between them and Cato.

In the opening scene of the play, Statilius reveals Cato's reputation as a "good" man:

Is his one life
On whom all good lives and their goods depend
In Rome's whole Empire, all the justice there
That's free and simple, all such virtues too,
And all such knowledge, nothing, nothing, all?[68]

Cato's advice to Statilius not to entertain a fear for either of their persons greater than that of the gods themselves then draws from the philosopher Athenodorus a comment that marks Cato's "goodness" as essentially Stoical:

Come, let him go, Statilius, and your fright;
This man hath inward guard past your young sight.[69]

When we learn further that Cato is a man whom neither "fair words" nor "rewards" can "corrupt,"[70] when we see that he can fearlessly defy Caesar in denying that either his or Pompey's army is needed to preserve order in Rome if only the conspirators are put to death, we know him at once as an independent spirit, whose devotion to the principles of right justifies his being a rational law unto himself. Like Chabot, Cato is not indifferent to the fate of others. Realizing that the loss of Caesar's men in the battle with Pompey is Pompey's loss as well,[71] he cautions Pompey to

Take pity on your country's blood as much
As possible may stand without the danger
Of hindering her justice on her foes.[72]

Nor does his friendship with Pompey interfere with his sense of duty. He remains as independent of Pompey as of Caesar. Risking his life in travels about the country on orders from the Senate, he forgoes the protection of Pompey's army, with the simple explanation: "My person is the least, my lord, I value."[73] This is the man whose character Chapman describes in the first four acts of *Caesar and Pompey.*

It will be remembered that Cicero in the *De Officiis* had advocated suicide as a duty under certain conditions: "Cato had been endowed by nature with an austerity beyond belief, and he himself had strengthened it by unswerving consistency and had remained ever true to his purpose and fixed resolve; and it was for him to die rather than to look upon the face of a tyrant."[74] This was the crisis in Catò's life that finally demanded Chapman's attention as well as Cicero's: Caesar has defeated Pompey, and he and his army are headed for Cato's home in Utica; Pompey has fled, and Cato is faced with almost certain disgrace at Caesar's hands. The fifth scene of Act IV opens showing Cato's son, Portius, removing a sword from the wall by Cato's bed. Portius orders a servant, Marcilius, to take "no note" of the action: Caesar is hastening to Utica to save Cato,

> Whom justly he suspects to be resolv'd
> Of any violence to his life, before
> He will preserve it by a tyrant's favour.[75]

Cato senses the fear in his son's mind, but refuses to think of asking Caesar to spare his life:

> I have ever been in every justice
> Better than Caesar, and was never conquer'd,
> Or made to fly for life, as Caesar was.
> But have been victor ever to my wish,
> Gainst whomsoever ever hath oppos'd . . .
> My fame affirm my life receiv'd from him!
> I'll rather make a beast my second father.[76]

Statilius, one of Cato's disciples,[77] also questions whether the true Roman should live to be a slave to a tyrant's power:

Why was man ever just but to be free
Gainst all injustice, and to bear about him
As well all means to freedom every hour,
As every hour he should be arm'd for death,
Which only is his freedom?[78]

When Athenodorus denies that man is free to elect death, "Till
nature or the law impose it on him,"[79] Cato attacks his belief with
arguments selected from Stoic doctrine:

                    All just men
Not only may enlarge their lives, but must,
From all rule tyrannous, or live unjust.[80]

Cato then goes on to defend his choosing death as the privilege of
every man "bound to justice":

            therefore not to serve injustice:
Justice itself ought ever to be free,
And therefore every just man being a part
Of that free justice, should be free as it.[81]

    But when Athenodorus continues to doubt that there is a "law
for death," Cato restates a belief Bussy had first expressed. Bussy
had argued that the man who was a law unto himself needed no
other law. Byron refined Bussy's statement to mean that he who was
a *rational* law unto himself needed no other law. It remained for
Cato finally to give this idea Stoic dignity:

            is not every just man to himself
The perfect'st law?[82]

When Athenodorus grants this hypothesis, Cato then begins to
drive home the whole Stoic argument in justification of suicide:

                              Then to himself
Is every just man's life subordinate.
Again, sir, is not our free soul infus'd
To every body in her absolute end
To rule that body? In which absolute rule
Is she not absolutely empress of it?
And being empress, may she not dispose
It, and the life in it, at her just pleasure?[83]

Athenodorus' objection to destroying life brings from Cato a final thrust that is the epitome of the Stoic's refusal to fight against anything his reason tells him he should accept:

                         No, she not destroys it
When she dislives it, that their freedoms may
Go firm together, like their powers and organs,
Rather than let it live a rebel to her.[84]

In his note on this philosophical discussion, Professor Parrott writes, "Chapman has . . . greatly expanded the argument [in Plutarch], and after putting into Cato's mouth a genuine stoical defense of suicide . . . goes on to a statement of views on the immortality and resurrection of the body which would have astounded any philosopher of classic times."[85] This part of the argument begins when, in answer to Cato's implication that death is not the end of man's life, Athenodorus offers in rebuttal the Stoic tenet that the body does not live once death has "reft it."[86] But Cato then introduces his belief in the resurrection, "man's second life," and Professor Parrott's statement that "there can be little doubt . . . that 11. 90-136 embody Chapman's interpretation and defense of the dogma of the resurrection,"[87] seems eminently correct.

The important thing, however, is that in what are almost his last words written on the Stoic approach to death, Chapman obviously finds the Stoic insistence on the finality of death insufficient for his own personal credo. In his Dedication to *The Revenge of Bussy D'Ambois,* he had already shown an inclination to embrace the Christian belief in a life after death when he wrote, "I make it matter of my faith, that we truly retain an intellectual feeling of good or bad after this life, proportionably answerable to the love or neglect we bear here to all virtue, and truly humane instruction."[88] In his attempt to harmonize Stoicism and Christianity, Chapman has added a Christian idea to pagan Stoicism in Cato's defense of the dogma of life after death.

Cato then refers to Nature that "works in all things to an end,"[89] to prove his argument. His reasoning, in the identical vein of Epictetus's words, "For nature mother of all things hath framed every man to some particular thing,"[90] leads him to conclude:

> therefore the mortality to which
> A man is subject rather is a sleep
> Than bestial death, since Sleep and Death are call'd
> The twins of Nature.[91]

Cato's introduction of Christian dogma has not erased the thought of suicide from his mind. While he admits that the possibility of a second life is "a good cheerful doctrine for good men,"[92] he remembers, too, that

> no life urgeth
> To any violence further than his owner
> And graver men hold fit,[93]

a recollection which fits his earlier emphasis on a just man's being his own perfect law. The scene closes with Cato's humble acknowledgment that his friends must not too readily embrace the reasoning that forces him to contemplate suicide:

> Statilius,
> My reasons must not strengthen you in error,
> Nor learn'd Athenodorus' gentle yielding.
> Talk with some other deep philosophers,
> Or some divine priest of the knowing gods,
> And hear their reasons.[94]

In the second scene of Act V we find Cato still thinking in terms of the just man and suicide. He fears his "resolution" to take his own life, for he now inclines to the belief that his life belongs to the law rather than to himself. But, since the law was "made for a sort of outlaws,"[95] he finds it impossible to yield himself to "public power":

> as if I could
> Be rack'd out of my veins to live in others,
> As so I must, if others rule my life,
> And public power keep all the right of death;
> As if men needs must serve the place of justice,
> The form and idol, and renounce itself,
> Ourselves, and all our rights in God and goodness,
> Our whole contents and freedoms, to dispose
> All in the joys and ways of arrant rogues![96]

The thought of putting his life in the hands of others being revolting to him, Cato sends for the sword that Portius has removed: he has determined to "pursue" his "reason," to allow no "soft-spleen'd servants" afraid of death to curb his desire "to conquer conquering Caesar." When both his physician and his servant refuse to bring him his sword, Cato calls for his son. Neither Portius' plea that his father remember his family nor Athenodorus' Stoic suggestion that he conform to the world since heaven itself cannot reform it can stay Cato. Again he calls for his sword. While waiting for the Page to bring it, Cato questions why Statilius and Brutus have disappeared. Statilius has gone "to serve the victor"; Brutus, too, has "gone to Caesar." At the mention of Brutus, Cato, turning to his son, advises him never to have anything to do with public affairs:

> But, for you, my son,
> However Caesar deals with me, be counsell'd
> By your experienc'd father not to touch
> At any action of the public weal,
> Nor any rule bear near her politic stern!
> For, to be upright and sincere therein
> Like Cato's son, the time's corruption
> Will never bear it.[97]

Then, like Clermont who faced death as a ship seeking a port on far-distant shores, Cato prepares to die with thoughts of immortality upon his lips:

> the Consuls' souls,
> That slew themselves so nobly, scorning life
> Led under tyrant's sceptres, mine would see.
> For we shall know each other, and past death
> Retain those forms of knowledge learn'd in life;
> Since, if what here we learn, we there shall lose,
> Our immortality were not life, but time.
> And that our souls in reason are immortal
> Their natural and proper objects prove;
> Which immortality and knowledge are.[98]

And Cato's last line, spoken as he rips out his entrails, is the consummation of Chapman's ideal for the Stoical man: "Just men are only free, the rest are slaves,"[99] a line that only states in a different way the words of the title page,

> Only a just man is a free man.

Whether in spite of the detailed stage directions in *Caesar and Pompey* we accept Chapman's own words, "Yet never touched it at the stage,"[100] or Professor Parrott's more likely theory, "It was nevertheless obtained by the players at Blackfriars and rehearsed for performance, at which time the directions would naturally be inserted,"[101] it is obvious that this, like other Chapman tragedies, belongs rather to the study than to the stage. Words again take precedence over action. It could not have been otherwise, however, for Chapman, always more interested in interpreting an action than in the action itself, had here undertaken to depict not just one hero, but three. In each of the preceding tragedies, he had focused on a single protagonist. Never before had Chapman forced that character to share his importance with more than one other figure, and then only for the purpose of contrast or comparison. The fact that he now found himself occupied with the development of three central characters called for such skill in dramatic construction as Chapman had seldom attained. The result was inevitable: the tragedy appears wanting in that kind of technique in which word naturally follows or accompanies action.

Although Caesar and Pompey play the title roles in this drama, neither of these protagonists attains the significance Chapman was accustomed to give the men whose names appear in the title. Caesar obviously emerges as third in importance, and Pompey does not entirely dominate the action. And yet Chapman has divided by far the greater number of scenes between these two men; furthermore, that division gives each character control of the same number of scenes. Cato, on the other hand, actually dominates only two scenes, yet his influence pervades the whole play. Cato achieves his pre-eminent role as *the* Stoic protagonist only because Chapman found it impossible to confine the true Stoical man to a minor role—not because of dramatic necessity, but simply because of his personal predilection for this arch example of the Stoical man. Though

Cato's rôle is pre-eminent, it is both noteworthy and ironical that Pompey achieves a tragic significance as singular in Chapman as it is effective, particularly since the dramatist has developed the character of Pompey to the point where his portrait is comparable to that of either Clermont or Chabot even before Cato becomes the leading figure in the tragedy in the final scene of Act IV.

But Chapman's decision "to make Cato the hero was, of course," as Spencer writes, "to make suicide its [the play's] subject."[102] As we noted in *The Revenge of Bussy,* Chapman introduced Clermont's suicide in the last scene of the play only after the murder of his friend, the Guise, and then devoted only fifty-four lines to it. In *Caesar and Pompey,* however, more than one hundred and fifty lines are devoted to a discussion of suicide on two different occasions. Clermont's decision to die has no relation whatsoever to his life prior to the moment of that decision; he thinks only in terms of the future; death has become for him the only act possible. Cato's resolve to take his own life, however, is inherent in his character. It springs from his inability to sacrifice his independent spirit to Caesar's tyranny. Only after he has decided that life can no longer provide him with both justice and freedom does he look forward to "the next world." As Spencer has stated, "the way his [Chapman's] hero expresses himself *is* original. . . . The medieval ideas are abandoned, and the Stoic beliefs, which were one of the chief symptoms of the Renaissance, are for the first time in popular literature thoroughly adopted and related to life."[103]

Yet no amount of logical analysis on the part of Cato as to the necessity of his suicide gives his death the kind of tragic meaning created by the death of Pompey. As in the case of Clermont, we experience no deep regret at Cato's death because the ethical structure of Stoicism has dictated a course of action which, as Battenhouse has stated, "makes of tragic catharsis a mockery."[104] Caesar's victory appears empty not because Cato has deliberately removed himself from the Emperor's power, but because there is no place in life for the man whose ethics prevents any compromise between principles and realities. Cato may well be the most complete Stoic Chapman ever created, but his very perfection in Stoic doctrine disqualifies him as a true protagonist of tragedy since the truly tragic hero denies evil only to vindicate good.

Chapman again runs the full gamut of Stoic ethics in *Caesar and Pompey,* drawing upon both the conventional patterns and the more specific tenets of the philosophy. And the drama supports the contention that when Chapman develops his tragic protagonists wholly within the confines of Stoic doctrine, he denies them the opportunity of achieving heroic stature. They remain forever incapable of inspiring others to resist adversity. Since Chapman's Stoical men maintain complete control over any circumstance that threatens to disrupt their mental peace, their lives are dedicated to those principles that culminate in the negation of tragedy.

EPILOGUE

A STUDY of the six tragedies comprising the Chapman canon shows clearly that the philosophy of Stoicism must remain a most important consideration in any attempt to explain the mind and art of his Jacobean playwright. Such a study suggests that the generally accepted chronology of these plays may not be wholly in keeping with the development of Chapman's interest in the Stoical man. Furthermore, the dramatist's predilection for the ethics of Stoicism emerges as the reason for his writing only one tragedy, *Bussy D'Ambois,* that has enjoyed lasting success and that continues to entitle Chapman to a reputation as a writer of great tragical drama.

Chapman's concern with Stoicism does not reflect itself only in the portraits of the great Stoic protagonists—Clermont, Pompey, and Cato. In all of his tragedies from *Bussy D'Ambois* through *Caesar and Pompey,* the Stoic ethics plays an increasingly prominent role. Though both Bussy and Byron are typical examples of the Renaissance hero, Chapman's early distrust of the man who would sacrifice the world to his own lust for power foreshadows the concept of the Stoical man to whom Chapman first pays respect in the character of the King in *The Tragedy of Byron.* Without Bussy and Byron, who stand in marked contrast to this King, Chapman could never have presented with such clear insight the psychology of Clermont, the man who chooses to live in accord with Stoic doctrine. Just as certainly Chabot owes his integrated adherence to the Stoic truths that shape his life to the fact that Chapman had earlier developed the character of Clermont as if determined that this "Senecal man" should talk and act in strict conformity with Stoic dogma. Because Chabot does not openly acknowledge his indebtedness to these Stoic doctrines, critics have been slow to realize the completely Stoical nature of this great arbiter of justice. Pompey and Cato, too, owe their Stoic individuality to the fact that Chapman had become completely devoted to the Stoic principles which we must believe dictated to a great extent his own reactions to a world in which high moral standards of conduct often seemed inoperative. The ethics of Stoicism, then, exerted an ever increasing influence on the development of the men to whom Chapman gave the major roles in the dramas he called "tragedies."

That this influence becomes more and more distinct as Chapman examines more and more carefully the moral intent of Bussy, Byron, and Clermont only strengthens the accepted chronology of the dramas in which they appear. It is also an indication that as an idea begins to dominate the artist's mind, the extent of its influence is reflected in his work. With Parrott's dating of *Bussy D'Ambois,* *The Conspiracy and Tragedy of Charles Duke of Byron,* and *The Revenge of Bussy D'Ambois,* then, there can be little room for disagreement. But despite Mrs. Solve's logical exposition of the thesis that *Chabot* is a topical play based on political incidents occurring in English history between the years 1621 and 1624, and Parrott's general agreement, the present writer adheres to the belief that *Chabot* dates originally from 1612. It seems unlikely that Chapman could have let so long a period of time elapse before reverting again to French history, from which he had derived his three earlier dramas, particularly when a source exists for *Chabot* in Pasquier's *Les Recherches de la France* of 1611. This contention is, of course, not altogether unanswerable, for it explains in no way the fact that this play was not entered in the Stationers' Registers until 1638 and that it was not published until 1639. It should be remembered, however, that the text we now have contains Shirley's hand as well as Chapman's. The date of approximately 1612 not only maintains the continuity of Chapman's interest in French history and the development of his art; it also establishes *Caesar and Pompey* as his last drama, written in 1612-13 against a background of Roman history, completely congenial both to the Stoic philosophy and to Chapman's strong inclination toward men like Pompey and Caesar whose lives symbolized the moral virtues of that philosophy.

The failure of Chapman's tragical dramas ever to achieve fully the stature of great tragedy is in great measure due to the fact that Stoicism negates the premises from which such tragedy develops. Mere chance did not determine that *Bussy D'Ambois,* Chapman's outstanding success in tragedy both on the stage and in the acclaim of literary history, proves to be the only play on which the ethics of Stoicism exerted so slight an influence. Because Chapman created Bussy as a Renaissance hero, an individualist who never invites comparison with any Stoical character as Byron invites it with the King who decides that he must die, Bussy appears as one of passion's slaves who bring about their own downfall by setting in motion a series of events they are powerless to control. The ensuing struggle of the individual against his environment *is* dramatic, and in this one play we have the first and only instance of real tragedy. When, however, Chapman approves in the two Byron plays the King whose rule follows a clearly defined and thoroughly Stoical conception of the responsibilities of kingship, and sends Byron, another hero cast in the Renaissance mold, to his death as retribution for aspiring to greatness, Stoicism has begun to establish the pattern that is to obtain in each of the following dramas. Already the ethics of Stoicism has created a world in which men like Byron have no place; Chapman no longer regards the fall of "great" men as a fitting subject for dramatic tragedy.

In the last three of his so-called tragedies, Chapman then selects "good" men like Clermont, Chabot, Pompey, and Cato as his protagonists, heroes whose lives are dominated by Stoicism, a system of ethics always devoid of drama in general[1] and of tragedy in particular. Clermont follows Stoical doctrines so closely that they seriously interfere with his avenging Bussy's death, and eventually lead him to commit suicide after the Guise's murder because the Guise provided his only excuse for living. Chabot lives in a wider world than Clermont, realizing fully the mutual obligations existing between him and society. But Chabot, too, proves himself unequal to the demands of life. He accepts death as the reward of him who has made the cause of justice the sole justification of his life. Pompey and Cato are likewise the victims of the Stoic ethics; Pompey becomes a good Stoic only to lose his life at the hands of Caesar's assassins, and Cato robs the world of his goodness, choosing suicide rather than Caesar's tyranny.

No other of Chapman's tragical dramas reflecting his growing interest in the ethics of Stoicism presents as provocative problems in interpretation as *The Tragedy of Caesar and Pompey*. Since it was Chapman's custom to name his tragedies for their central figure, why did he not call this play *The Tragedy of Cato*, or why, at least, did he not place the name of Cato in the title? Always before, Chapman had focused the attention of his audience where that attention belonged. Even Clermont bears the D'Ambois name. But he calls this drama *The Tragedy of Caesar and Pompey*, although it is Cato rather than either Caesar or Pompey who lingers in our minds as he lingered in Chapman's own. Did Chapman, faced with three historical figures whose personal histories were closely interrelated, select the names of the two men his audience would know best? Or had Chapman—we venture to ponder—become as fully aware as we have that *The Tragedy of Cato* would have been no tragedy at all, since Cato faced death not like the ordinary man but like a Stoic? Was Chapman aware that in his own engrossing interest in the more-than-human philosopher, who lived his philosophy, he had reached the end inevitable in his own philosophy and artistic development—the negation of tragedy?

Did he realize that the artist in him had become overlaid by the thinker? Not only in the negation of tragedy does this play fall short of greatness, for in the playwright's attempt to preserve in dramatic form the tragedy of the lives of both Caesar and Pompey for his audience at the same time that he glorified the Stoicism of Cato to satisfy his own interest, Chapman so dissipated his energies that the play lacks unity as it lacks true tragedy.

The Tragedy of Caesar and Pompey is provocative, too, because of the fact that Chapman bolsters Cato's pagan defense of suicide with the Christian doctrine of the Resurrection. This joining together of alien ideologies may be more easily explained than the omission of Cato's name from the title of the play. It is quite probable that Chapman realized he was writing his last drama about the Stoical man. Though he himself had learned to think as a Stoic, there can be little doubt as one studies his entire literary work that Chapman was indeed a Christian. He was, therefore, unable to refrain from adding his personal belief in a life after death to Cato's Stoical justification of suicide, incongruous though such a combination might be. Chapman knew as well as we that these two ideas represented sharply opposed points of view, yet he joined them simply because the finality with which Stoicism regarded death did not meet his own personal credo.

All of the Stoical heroes portrayed by Chapman only acquiesce in the events that make struggle against the actualities of life both unnecessary and ineffective. As the playwright adapts Stoicism more and more to his dramatic purposes, his art exhibits a proportionate decline in tragic power that results finally in the negation of tragedy.

APPENDIX A: THE TRAGEDY OF ALPHONSUS EMPEROR OF GERMANY

ALTHOUGH Parrott included *The Tragedy of Alphonsus Emperor of Germany* in his edition of *The Tragedies of George Chapman,* he did not believe that it was a Chapman play: "The only certainty that I can offer the reader is a negative, that Chapman does not appear to have had any connexion with its composition."[1] Nor did he believe that this tragedy was wholly Peele's: "The most that we can grant Peele is, I think, to admit the possibility that he, perhaps in collaboration with another author, composed an old play on this subject, which has been subjected to so thorough a revision as to leave only a few traces of his hand."[2] To account "for the knowledge it reveals of German life and manners, and for its frequent and idiomatic use of the German language,"[3] Parrott wrote, "such a collaborator, not in the original composition of the play, but in the revision which I have assumed, might, I believe, be found in the person of Rudolpf Weckherlin."[4] Since 1910, succeeding scholars have investigated further the problems which Parrott's work suggested.

In 1916, Sykes concurred in Parrott's decision that this tragedy was not the work of Chapman: "Now nothing can be more certain, if external evidence counts for anything at all, than that Chapman could not possibly have been the author of *Alphonsus, Emperor of Germany.*"[5] But Sykes concluded, after assigning it "a date within a few years of 1590,"[6] that the play is Peele's: "When its language is examined and compared with Peele's acknowledged works we shall find conclusive evidence—and that of a kind which cannot be supposed to have attracted the attention of any seventeenth-century writer or compiler of catalogues—that it is his."[7]

Dowling, however, in 1933 again associated Chapman's name with this tragedy and retained the idea of a German collaborator when he wrote, "I believe that the original play was wholly or in part by Peele, incorrectly called "John Poole" in the Stationers' Register entry; that it was rewritten for royal performance by Chapman [before 1634],[8] and that he was assisted in this revision by a German collaborator."[9]

In the same year Bowers developed his discussion of the problem without reference to either Peele or Chapman, contending,

> (1) that Weckherlin was certainly not the reviser of the play for a court performance in 1636 before the Elector Palatine, and, indeed, that the play cannot safely be identified with the *Alfonso* acted on that occasion; (2) that the play was written by one man in the complete form in which we know it, and has not undergone revision by another dramatist; (3) that the date of composition can be assigned to the years 1594-99 (and probably to 1597-99).[10]

The present writer agrees with most critics that neither Chapman's hand nor his mind can be detected in this tragedy; he finds nothing in the play characteristic of the dramatist's established ideas and attitudes.

APPENDIX B: REVENGE FOR HONOUR

SINCE 1910, when Professor Parrott accepted "as quite discredited the idea that Chapman was in any way concerned with *Revenge for Honour*,"[1] no critic has argued for retaining this play in the Chapman canon. On the other hand, Parrott's conclusion, "We may then identify it with *The Parricide*, and assume that play to have been written by 'an apt and gifted pupil of Fletcher's,' and to have been revised, either for the stage or for the press, by Glapthorne,"[2] has not been wholly accepted by later critics. In 1916 Sykes definitely attributed the play to Glapthorne: "It requires, however, no very close study of Glapthorne's acknowledged work to show that it [*Revenge for Honour*] is his."[3] In 1937, Walter followed Sykes in making the same ascription: "It was written by Glapthorne alone about 1640 or between that date and the closing of the theatres."[4] And, in 1938, Shaver differed with Walter only in giving a wider latitude to this date of composition: "*Revenge for Honour* . . . seems to have been written by Glapthorne sometime between 1627 and 1641."[5]

If any valid reason existed for giving further credence to Marriott's claim, made in 1654,[6] that Chapman was the author of *Revenge for Honour*, it should reveal itself in the influence of the Stoic ethics upon this tragedy. While a re-examination of this play does indicate some knowledge of Stoical doctrines, it yields no substantial body of such evidence. And the author does not rely on this knowledge of Stoicism, as Chapman was accustomed to do, for the development of his material.

For example, Tarifa, Abilqualit's tutor, scorns carnal pleasure. In lines that do not necessarily derive from Stoic doctrine, he tells the Prince,

> 'Tis most ignoble that a mind, unshaken
> By fear, should by a vain desire be broken
> Or that those powers no labour e'er could vanquish,
> Should be o'ercome and thrall'd by sordid pleasure.[7]

But Abilqualit, in spite of his respect for Reason, refuses to be governed by any such moral scruples:

> Why should I
> Put off my reason, valour, honour, virtue,
> In hopes to gain a beauty, whose possession
> Renders me more uncapable of peace
> Than I am now I want it? . . .
> Idle fool,
> There is no law but what's prescribed by love,
> Nature's first moving organ; nor can aught
> What Nature dictates to us be held vicious.[8]

Here, the Prince's denial of Reason in favor of passion is as complete a distortion of Stoic doctrine as is his twisting of the Stoic concept of nature to excuse his personal deviation from her laws. Likewise, Abilqualit's determination,

> I'm resolved, let what
> Happen what will, I'll stand it, and defend
> Caropia's honour, though mine own I ruin,[9]

indicates to how great an extent the Stoic acquiescence in Destiny has been enervated: it has become a valid reason for persisting in an unethical action. Consequently, his statement, "Nor repine/ I at my destiny,"[10] lacks the significance of the true Stoic's respect for Fate. Nor does the typical Stoic and Christian sentiment which ends the play, "They're only truly great wh' are truly good,"[11] in any way indicate Chapman's association with *Revenge for Honour,* for the action of the play is lacking that ethical force which would make the line seem a fitting moral conclusion.

In short, though there are evidences of Stoic influence in *Revenge for Honour,* the author's use of this material is such that there can be no reason for linking Chapman's name with the writing of this tragedy.

APPENDIX C: POSSIBLE SOURCES OF CHAPMAN'S KNOWLEDGE OF STOICISM

MONSIEUR SCHOELL in his definitive study, *Études sur L'Human-isme Continental en Angleterre*,[1] has demonstrated in a most concrete fashion the sources of much of Chapman's knowledge of Stoicism. From the 1563 Latin edition of Hieronymus Wolfius,[2] Chapman derived his knowledge of Epictetus; here he found the *Manual (Enchiridion), Arrian's Discourses of Epictetus,* the *Fragments,* and the *Commentaries of Simplicius.* However, Chapman need not have gone to Wolfius to find a text of Epictetus, for just four years after this edition, there was published in England the first English translation by James Sanford of at least some of his work.[3] And Miss Bartlett's statement that Chapman's reading of Epictetus was concentrated in the years 1611-12,[4] makes it possible that Chapman knew and used Healey's translation, *Epictetus His Manuell and Cebes His Table,* either the first edition published in England in 1610 or the second of the same year.[5]

Sanford's translation of the *Manual* is a far more interesting, if not more important, document than Healey's more literal one of 1610, for Sanford's, from the French "out of Greek" and "conferred with two Latine Translations," is something more than just another translation. By the nature of its dedication to the "virtuous Princesse, *Elizabeth* by the grace of God, England, Fraunce and Ireland Queene, defender of the faith," of its preface *To the Reader* in which Sanford translates the Greek title of *Enchyridion* as signifying "a short Dagger" to recommend the little book as one which would save the reader "from the filthy fogge of wicked vices," and of its insertions of frequent personal *Marginal Notes* and *Annotations* to the various chapter numbers or captions, the

Sanford translation becomes a typical example of one kind of humanistic conduct book so popular in the Renaissance. So much does it differ in both context and appearance from P. E. Matheson's translation in the volume edited by Oates[6] that the reader cannot help wondering at first sight if they are, as purported, translations of one and the same work. Furthermore, Sanford's English version of the *Manual* is so near in spirit to Chapman's seeming understanding of Stoic doctrine that one is tempted to believe that much of Chapman's knowledge of Stoicism came directly from Sanford's work.

Schoell has also indicated conclusively that Chapman knew and used, particularly between 1608 and 1614, and perhaps even during his whole lifetime, Xylander's Latin translation of Plutarch's *Moralia*.[7] Even though Chapman seems not to have known Philemon Holland's *The Philosophie, Commonlie Called "the Morals,"* it was, nevertheless, translated and published in England in 1603. Schoell's evidence, which would seem to demonstrate in Chapman's use of both Epictetus and Plutarch his preference for a Latin work even when an English translation was available, indicates not only the preference but also the ease with which he worked in Latin, an ease which seems not to have extended to Greek.

A third author from whom Chapman derived his ideas of Stoicism and to whom Schoell devotes attention is Erasmus.[8] Chapman's use of *The Adages* extends beyond *The Iliad,* for references to Erasmus can be noted in the tragedies that are not actually named as they are in *The Iliad.* Again, there is no reason why Chapman could not have read *The Adages* in English as well as in the original Latin, for the work was published in English in 1539 by Richard Tavener, succeeding editions of the same work appearing in 1539, 1545, 1550, 1552, and 1569, respectively. In 1542, Nicholas Udall translated the *Apophthegmes, That Is to Saie, Prompte Saiynges: First Gathered by Erasmus;* this edition was followed by a second in 1564. In 1540, Tavener also published *Apothegmata, Selections: Flores aliquot sententiarum ex variis collecti scriptoribus,* in both Latin and English, a work which went into a second edition in the same year, and appeared again in 1547, 1550, and 1556(?).

No literal translation of the works of Marcus Aurelius appeared in English until Casaubon's of 1633, but between the years 1535 and 1596 there appeared no fewer than thirteen editions of *The Golden Boke of Marcus Aurelius,* translated by J. Bourchier, Lord Barners, from the work of Antonio de Guevara who did not pretend to give a literal translation of the author of the *Meditations.* Apparently, then, Chapman read this neo-Stoic in a Latin translation of Continental origin.

If Chapman did not choose to read his Cicero in books of similar origin, there were available to him numerous editions published in England, both in Latin and English. In 1579, Cicero's *De Officiis, de Senectute, de Amicitia, Paradoxa, Somniu Scipionis* appeared in the original Latin, followed by other editions in 1595 and 1614, which Chapman may have known and used. The same work, *Foure Seuerall Treatises: Conteyninge Discourses of Frendshippe, Old Age, Paradoxes, and Scipio His Dreame,* was published in 1577. The *de Amicitia,* published as a separate work, had been printed as early as 1530(?); another edition of the work appeared in 1550, with a second in 1562. The *Epistolae familiares* was published first in England in 1570, followed by successive editions in 1574, 1575, 1579, 1585, 1591, and 1602, respectively. Obviously, Chapman had easy access to several editions of Cicero whose works we know to have been popular in the sixteenth century for their highly ethical character.

Since Thomas Lodge's *The Workes of L. A. Seneca, Both Morall a. Naturall,* did not appear until 1614, although editions of the plays in English before this date had been variously published, it would seem mandatory to believe that Chapman's knowledge of

The Epistles must have been obtained from a foreign edition which had come to his hands.

It is also possible that Chapman knew two other works which related to Stoicism. In 1598, Guillaume Du Vair's *The Moral Philosophie of the Stoicks* was published in England, and Justus Lipsius' *De Constantia libri duo* appeared in 1596, a work with strong Stoic leanings translated by J. Stradling in 1595 under the title *Two Bookes of Constancie.*

It is evident from this brief survey of the works of the foremost Stoic authors, published both on the Continent and in England in Latin, French, Spanish, and English, that Chapman had ample opportunity to read in the philosophy of Stoicism. And while it is helpful from one point of view to know in some instances just what books Chapman used, it is even more interesting to note that the world in which Chapman lived had a real and lively interest in Stoicism, an interest that was supplied by not infrequent editions of works whose context had a strong ethical content or bias.

NOTES

PROLOGUE

1. For a full account of the number and variety of their works, see Appendix C. As Zeller has indicated, both Cicero and Plutarch "may be considered as authorities at second hand for the teaching of the Stoics." Eduard Zeller, *The Stoics, Epicureans, and Sceptics,* trans. Oswald J. Reichel, p. 53.

2. Epictetus, *The Manuel of Epictetus,* etc., trans. Ia. Sanford.

3. Guillaume Du Vair, *The Moral Philosophie of the Stoicks,* trans. T. I., pp. A5r and A6v.

4. Thomas Lodge, *The Workes of Lvcivs Annaevs Seneca.*

5. Seneca, *Seneca ad Lucilium Epistulae Morales,* trans. Richard M. Gummere, II, 9-11.

6. *Ibid.,* p. 447. "The happy life depends upon this and this alone: our attainment of perfect reason."

7. *Ibid.,* I, 255.

8. *Ibid.,* III, 229.

9. Epictetus, "Manual," *The Stoic and Epicurean Philosophers,* ed. Whitney J. Oates, p. 480.

10. Seneca, III, 351.

11. *Ibid.,* p. 343.

12. *Ibid.,* I, 93.

13. *Ibid.,* II, 23.

14. *Ibid.,* p. 3.

15. Epictetus, *Discourses,* ed. Whitney J. Oates, p. 230.

16. Seneca, II, 21.

17. Marcus Aurelius, *Meditations,* ed. Whitney J. Oates, p. 539.

18. Cicero, *De Senectute,* trans. William Armistead Falconer, p. 51.

19. Seneca, I, 409-11.

20. Epictetus, *Discourses,* p. 242.

21. Plutarch, *Moralia,* trans. Frank Cole Babbitt, II, 113, 119.

22. Epictetus, *Discourses,* p. 225.

23. Epictetus, *Manual,* trans. Sanford, p. 21v.

24. *Ibid.,* p. 2v. "If thẽ onely thou decline that which is not agreable be the nature of the things whiche are in us, thou shalt neuer chaunce into that, whiche thou shalt flee."

25. Seneca, III, 377.

26. *Ibid.,* pp. 49, 59.

27. Marcus Aurelius, *Meditations,* pp. 541, 563.

28. Epictetus, *Discourses,* p. 470.

29. Seneca, III, 105-07.

30. Epictetus, *Discourses,* p. 449.

31. *Ibid.,* p. 414.

32. Cicero, *De Amicitia,* trans. William Armistead Falconer, p. 131.

33. *Ibid.,* p. 163.

34. Epictetus, *Manual,* trans. Sanford, pp. 6v and 6r. "A single person (if other things be correspondent) may be in his life time, cõtented with a little, and die with a more pacient minde. A wife, children, and familie, do more trouble and disquiete the husbande and father, being as well in good healthe, as sicke, than his life."

35. Seneca, I, 17.

36. Plutarch, II, 157.

37. Seneca, I, 325.

38. Epictetus, *Discourses,* p. 226.

39. Seneca, II, 73.

40. *Ibid.,* I, 409.

41. *Ibid.*

42. Cicero, *De Officiis,* trans. Walter Miller, p. 115.

43. Zeller, *The Stoics, Epicureans, and Sceptics,* p. 400.

CHAPTER ONE

In *Bussy D'Ambois* Chapman tells the story of Bussy's rise and fall. Discontented with his lot, Bussy comes under the influence of Monsieur, the King's brother, an aspirant to the Crown. When Monsieur introduces him at Court, Bussy not only becomes the King's favorite but also the lover of Tamyra, Count Montsurry's wife. Because he suspects that Bussy is now interested only in advancing himself, Monsieur plots his revenge. He discovers the affair between Tamyra and Bussy and reveals it to Montsurry. Monsieur and Montsurry then hire assassins, who ambush and finally murder Bussy in Montsurry's house.

1. Thomas Marc Parrott, *The Tragedies of George Chapman,* p. 541.
2. Thomas Marc Parrott, *The Comedies of George Chapman,* p. 890.
3. *Ibid.,* p. 895.
4. *Ibid.,* p. 897.
5. Phyllis B. Bartlett, *The Poems of George Chapman,* p. 448.
6. Parrott, *Tragedies,* p. 541.
7. *Ibid.,* p. 591.
8. *Ibid.,* p. 571.
9. *Ibid.,* p. 655.
10. *Ibid.,* p. 632. The date, 1624, is the *terminus ad quem* advanced by Norma Dobie Solve in her *Stuart Politics in Chapman's "Tragedy of Chabot,"* p. 62.
11. Francis Meres, "Palladis Tamia, Wits Treasury," 1598, *Elizabethan Critical Essays,* ed. G. Gregory Smith (Oxford, 1904), II, 320. Chapman is listed among "the best Poets for Comedy."
12. Parrott, *Tragedies,* p. 569, n. 201.
13. Meres, "Palladis Tamia," II, 319. Chapman is listed as early as 1598 among "our best for Tragedie."

14. Parrott, *Tragedies,* p. 543.

15. *Ibid.*

16. Howard Baker, *Induction to Tragedy,* p. 198.

17. Henry Burrowes Lathrop, *Translations from the Classics into English from Caxton to Chapman, 1477-1620,* p. 139.

18. T. S. Eliot, "Seneca in Elizabethan Translation," *Selected Essays 1917-1932,* p. 75.

19. F. L. Lucas, *Seneca and Elizabethan Tragedy,* p. 127.

(All references to Chapman's tragedies are from the Parrott edition.)

20. *Bussy D'Ambois,* II, 2, 34: "Dames maritorious ne'er were meritorious."

21. III, 2, 288-92.

22. ll. 297-98, 304-05.

23. IV, 1, 15-21.

24. l. 126.

25. V, 1, 62-68. (Italics mine.)

26. ll. 83-88.

27. ll. 100-02.

28. V, 4, 204-08.

29. F. S. Boas, *Bussy D'Ambois and the Revenge of Bussy D'Ambois,* p. xxii.

30. James Smith, "George Chapman," *Scrutiny,* IV (1935-36), 53.

31. *Bussy D'Ambois,* I, 1, 46-50.

32. ll. 32-33.

33. ll. 76-81.

34. ll. 84-85.

35. ll. 128-30.

36. V, 4, 147.

37. I, 1, 222.

38. I, 2, 85-86.

39. l. 110.

40. l. 152.

41. ll. 157-65.

42. II, 1, 150-51.

43. ll. 174-79.

44. ll. 203-04. (See also n. 87.)

45. III, 2, 83-87.

46. ll. 88-97.

47. V, 4, 147.

48. III, 2, 423-58.

49. ll. 441-42.

50. ll. 456-58.

51. V, 4; 84-99, 102, 107-11. (Italics mine.)

52. Hardin Craig, *The Enchanted Glass,* the Elizabethan Mind in literature, pp. 84, 136.

53. Parrott, *Tragedies,* p. 546.

54. Richard H. Perkinson, "Nature and the Tragic Hero in Chapman's Bussy Plays," *Modern Language Quarterly,* III (1942), 269.

55. Theodore Spencer, *Death and Elizabethan Tragedy,* p. 243.

56. Havelock Ellis, *Chapman,* p. 30.

57. Parrott, *Tragedies,* p. 545.

58. Hardin Craig, "Ethics in the Jacobean Drama: the Case of Chapman," *The Parrott Presentation Volume,* ed. Hardin Craig, p. 32.

59. *Bussy D'Ambois,* I, 1, 3-4.

60. ll. 10-13.

61. ll. 18-19.

62. ll. 28-33.

63. ll. 61-62.

64. ll. 113-17.

65. ll. 129-30.
66. ll. 138-43.
67. II, 2, 115-16.
68. III, 1, 117.
69. III, 2, 98-102.
70. *Revenge for Honour,* I, 1, 400.
71. *Bussy D'Ambois,* III, 1, 62-67.
72. Parrott, *Tragedies,* p. 546.
73. *Ibid.*
74. *Bussy D'Ambois,* IV, 1, 109-17.
75. V, 3, 11.
76. ll. 61-67.
77. ll. 70-74.
78. V, 4, 39-40.
79. ll. 73-74.
80. ll. 76-78.
81. ll. 131-34.
82. ll. 141-46.
83. See Willard Farnham, *The Medieval Heritage of Eliza-bethan Tragedy,* for a full discussion of the concept of Fortune at work in early English drama.
84. *Bussy D'Ambois,* I, 1, 41-42.
85. Perkinson, "Nature and the Tragic Hero," p. 269.
86. *Busssy D'Ambois,* II, 1, 190-94.
87. ll. 194-204.
88. V, 2; 1-4, 7-15.
89. ll. 21-31.
90. ll. 32-36.
91. ll. 41-44.
92. ll. 46-53.
93. Perkinson, "Nature and the Tragic Hero," pp. 266, 269.
94. *Ibid.,* p. 270.

95. Smith, "George Chapman," p. 45.
96. Parrott, *Tragedies,* p. 544.

CHAPTER TWO

In *The Conspiracy* Chapman relates the story of a historical situation at the Court of Henry of Navarre where Byron falls under the influence of the Duke of Savoy. The Duke, leagued with Spain against France, has come to the French Court to recruit discontented spirits for that cause. La Fin and Byron having been recommended to him as two such men, Savoy draws them into the plot against Henry. But Henry discovers the conspiracy and reveals his knowledge of it to Byron. At the end of the play, Byron on bended knee acknowledges his guilt to Henry, who forgives him.

The Tragedy resumes the story of Byron's conspiracy. The effect of the King's denunciation has been short-lived, and Byron has renewed his plotting. With documentary evidence of Byron's guilt, Henry seeks to persuade Byron by means of several messengers to return to Court from Dijon, where his duties as a soldier have taken him. Byron steadfastly refuses until one of his own captains, La Brunel, arrives with the false news that the conspiracy in which both Byron and La Fin are deeply involved remains undiscovered at Court. But La Fin has betrayed his coplotter, and Byron is placed under guard shortly after his return to Court. At his trial for treason, he unsuccessfully defends himself, and the death sentence is fulfilled with Byron's execution.

1. Parrott, *Tragedies,* p. 591.
2. *Ibid.*
3. *The Conspiracy,* II, 2, 25-31.
4. ll. 89-92.
5. ll. 93, 102-05.

6. III, 3, 24-30.

7. IV, 1, 176-85.

8. I, 2, 89-94.

9. III, 2, 277-79.

10. IV, 1, 93-100.

11. I, 1, 161.

12. II, 1, 83-87.

13. V, 2; 1, 28-29.

14. ll. 29-32.

15. ll. 33-34.

16. I, 1, 61-69.

17. ll. 79-82.

18. l. 83.

19. Epictetus, *Discourses*, p. 261.

20. *The Conspiracy*, I, 1, 95-96.

21. ll. 132-33, 137-41. (Italics mine.)

22. ll. 151-54, 156.

23. I, 2; 28-32, 35-37.

24. ll. 60-62.

25. III, 3, 112-14.

26. ll. 130-45. (Italics mine.)

27. V, 1, 83-85.

28. V, 2, 79-84.

29. Grimeston's *General Inventory;* see Parrott, *Tragedies,* pp. 593 ff.

30. *The Tragedy,* I, 1, 1.

31. l. 21.

32. ll. 55-57.

33. ll. 88-90.

34. *The Conspiracy,* II, 1, 90-91.

35. *The Tragedy,* I, 1, 106.

36. ll. 141-44.

37. V, 1, 49-65:

> if, because
> We sit above the danger of the laws,
> We likewise lift our arms above their justice,
> And that our heavenly Sovereign bounds not us
> In those religious confines out of which
> Our justice and our true laws are inform'd,
> In vain have we expectance that our subjects
> Should not as well presume to offend their earthly,
> As we our heavenly Sovereign; and this breach
> Made in the forts of all society,
> Of all celestial, and humane respects,
> Makes no strengths of our bounties, counsels, arms,
> Hold out against their treasons; and the rapes
> Made of humanity and religion,
> In all men's more than Pagan liberties,
> Atheisms, and slaveries, will derive their springs
> From their base precedents, copied out of kings.

38. I, 3, 30.
39. IV, 2, 45-47.
40. ll. 221-25.
41. III, 1, 1-2.
42. ll. 10-12.
43. ll. 140-42.
44. ll. 205-08.
45. III, 2, 78-79.
46. Parrott, *Tragedies,* p. 596. "Like Henry, Byron is a heightened and idealized representative of his class, the great warrior noble of the Renaissance."
47. *The Conspiracy,* I, 1, 151.
48. *The Tragedy,* IV, 1, 1.

49. ll. 6-10.
50. ll. 133-35.
51. IV, 2, 31-33.
52. ll. 63-65.
53. *The Conspiracy*, I, 2, 43-44.
54. ll. 154-64.
55. Spencer, *Death and Elizabethan Tragedy*, p. 245: "The fifth act of *Byron's Tragedy* . . . is the most complete presentation of a reaction to death in all Elizabethan drama."
56. *The Tragedy*, I, 3, 38.
57. III, 2, 121-22.
58. IV, 1, 38-41.
59. IV, 2, 1-4.
60. l. 7.
61. ll. 202-09.
62. l. 212.
63. ll. 309-11.
64. V, 1, 109-11.
65. l. 129.
66. V, 2, 168-69.
67. l. 184.
68. ll. 186-87.
69. l. 216.
70. ll. 288-89.
71. l. 305.
72. V, 3, 38-40. (Italics mine.)
73. l. 89.
74. ll. 139-42, 147.
75. V, 4, 20.
76. ll. 26-28.
77. ll. 32, 38.
78. ll. 40, 44.

79. ll. 52-55.

80. ll. 67-68.

81. ll. 73-74.

82. ll. 144-45.

83. ll. 161-62.

84. l. 183.

85. l. 228.

86. Spencer, *Death and Elizabethan Tragedy*, p. 251.

87. Farnham, *The Medieval Heritage of Elizabethan Tragedy*, pp. 188-93.

88. *Ibid.*, p. 191.

89. *Ibid.*, p. 193.

90. *Ibid.*

91. Parrott (*Tragedies*, p. 595) points out that the characterization of the King and the Duke "is effected much more by speeches than by action."

92. *The Conspiracy*, I, 2, 31.

93. *The Tragedy*, I, 1, 21.

94. *Bussy D'Ambois*, IV, 1, 114.

95. Parrott, *Tragedies*, pp. 595-96. "Henry is the type of the New Monarchy which rose out of the ruin of the Renaissance in the anarchy of the Wars of Religion, a monarchy national in origin, absolute by principle. But he is something more than a mere representative of the New Monarchy, he is the ideal monarch, as Chapman conceived him, the Patriot King."

96. *Ibid.*, p. 598. "*Bussy* and the *Revenge of Bussy* show . . . that the peculiar tragic theme of Chapman is the conflict of the individual with his environment and the inevitable issue of that conflict in the individual's defeat."

CHAPTER THREE

In *The Revenge of Bussy D'Ambois* Chapman devotes only a part of the slender dramatic action to the revenge of Bussy's murder by Clermont D'Ambois, a nonhistorical character created for the purpose. Of almost equal importance to the plot is the resentment that the King holds for Clermont. Believing that Clermont aspires to the Crown, the King sends him to Cambrai that Baligny may there take him into custody without interference from the Guise, Clermont's friend. A major portion of the play simply explores various Stoic doctrines in which Chapman had become deeply interested. In the final act of the drama, the King's Guard murders the Guise, Clermont kills Montsurry, thereby avenging Bussy's murder, and Clermont commits suicide.

1. Parrott, *Tragedies,* p. 571.
2. Bartlett, *The Poems of George Chapman,* p. 448.
3. Parrott, *Tragedies,* p. 77.
4. *The Revenge of Bussy D'Ambois,* I, 1, 335. See Parrott, *Tragedies,* p. 579, for a note on this line.
5. Bartlett, *The Poems of George Chapman,* p. 86.
6. *The Revenge of Bussy D'Ambois,* I, 1, 318.
7. ll. 319-22.
8. l. 354. (See Parrott's note, p. 579.)
9. Parrott, *Tragedies,* p. 571.
10. *Ibid.*
11. *Ibid.*
12. *Ibid.,* p. 573.
13. II, 1, 242.
14. I, 1, 1-4.
15. II, 1, 84-90.
16. III, 2, 94.
17. Parrott, *Tragedies,* p. 573.

18. III, 2, 96.
19. ll. 97-100.
20. ll. 109-16.
21. I, 1, 79-82.
22. V, 1, 107-20.
23. V, 3, 46.
24. *Byron's Tragedy,* I, 3, 1-3.
25. Parrott, *Tragedies,* p. 612, note to I, 3, 2-3.
26. *Byron's Tragedy,* III, 1, 54.
27. IV, 2, 139-40.
28. *Ibid.,* Chapman may have been recalling Plutarch's statement, IV, 415, in which he states that Alexander "confirms the truth of that principle of the Stoics which declares that every act which the wise man performs is an activity in accord with every virtue."
29. ll. 148-53.
30. V, 1, 78-79.
31. *The Revenge of Bussy D'Ambois,* II, 1, 201.
32. ll. 206-07.
33. ll. 216-19.
34. l. 223.
35. ll. 233-34.
36. V, 1, 60.
37. ll. 69-76.
38. I, 1, 61-65.
39. ll. 65-69.
40. ll. 170-72.
41. II, 1, 84-85.
42. ll. 97-104.
43. III, 2, 20-22.
44. Bartlett, *The Poems of George Chapman,* p. 49.
45. *Ibid.,* p. 327.

46. *The Revenge of Bussy D'Ambois,* IV, 4, 15.

47. I, 1, 25.

48. ll. 185-86.

49. II, 1, 144-46.

50. III, 1, 25.

51. ll. 29-30, 35-38.

52. III, 2, 37.

53. Percy Simpson, *The Theme of Revenge in Elizabethan Tragedy* (Annual Shakespeare Lecture of the British Academy), "Proceedings of the British Academy," XXI, 24.

54. *The Revenge of Bussy D'Ambois,* V, 1, 5.

55. ll. 29-32.

56. ll. 177-81.

57. III, 4, 66-75.

58. IV, 1, 131-45.

59. III, 4, 159-65.

60. IV, 4, 44.

61. III, 4, 48-50.

62. I, 1, 310-12.

63. II, 1, 5, 7.

64. I, 1, 153-58.

65. II, 1, 106-07.

66. l. 32.

67. l. 112.

68. l. 109.

69. III, 1, 16.

70. III, 2, 205.

71. IV, 3, 46.

72. ll. 61-66.

73. ll. 79-83.

74. I, 1, 152.

75. ll. 153-55. (Italics mine.)

76. III, 4, 136-41. (Italics mine.) See Parrott's note, p. 584, to III, 4, 127.

77. ll. 159-61.

78. IV, 5, 13.

79. V, 1, 150.

80. IV, 3, 104-06.

81. Epictetus, *Manual,* trans. Sanford, p. 11v.

82. *The Revenge of Bussy D'Ambois,* V, 5, 146-47.

83. Thomas Marc Parrott and Robert Hamilton Ball, *A Short View of Elizabethan Drama,* p. 102.

84. *The Revenge of Bussy D'Ambois,* I, 1, 146.

85. II, 1, 80-82.

86. ll. 269-77.

87. V, 1, 167-68.

88. ll. 186-88.

89. V, 5, 157-60.

90. ll. 200-01.

91. l. 206.

92. I, 2, 38-48. It should be pointed out that there is no external evidence of Chapman's ever having married, or of his having devoted himself exclusively to any male friend.

93. III, 1, 49-51.

94. ll. 51-52.

95. V, 1, 154-55.

96. ll. 159-60.

97. ll. 170-71, 182-85.

98. III, 4, 29-31.

99. ll. 32-33.

100. V, 4, 21.

101. V, 5, 162-67.

102. ll. 170-73.

103. Spencer, *Death and Elizabethan Tragedy,* p. 251.

104. Laurens J. Mills, *One Soul in Bodies Twain,* p. 309.

105. *Ibid.*

106. Spencer, *Death and Elizabethan Tragedy,* p. 252.

107. Smith, "George Chapman," p. 61.

108. *The Revenge of Bussy D'Ambois,* IV, 5, 4-13.

109. Smith, "George Chapman," p. 61.

110. *The Revenge of Bussy D'Ambois,* V, 5, 209.

111. James Smith, "George Chapman," *Scrutiny,* III (1934-35), 340.

CHAPTER FOUR

In the opening scenes of *Chabot,* Chapman presents the Admiral and the young Constable. Having become reconciled at the King's request, these two resolve to keep their pact "pure and inviolable." But the ambitious Chancellor causes one of the Constable's bills to be presented to Chabot for signature. The Admiral, finding the bill unjust, refuses to sign and tears the bill before returning it to the King. When Chabot defends his action, the King decides that his defense is insolent, and orders the Chancellor to examine Chabot's record. To charges that a court of law at first refuses to recognize, the Chancellor finally forces the judges' signatures. The King is pleased that Chabot's boldness has been condemned, for he may now pardon his faithful and loyal subject. But Chabot refuses the pardon on the grounds that he has been judged guilty of offenses he never committed. The King is impressed with his confidence, the judges are given an opportunity to describe how they were forced to defeat justice, and the Chancellor is arrested. Chabot, crushed by the injustice of the charges, dies, asking that the Chancellor be forgiven.

1. Parrott, *Tragedies,* p. 632.

2. *Ibid.,* p. 631.

3. *Ibid.*

4. *Ibid.*, p. 632.

5. *Ibid.*, p. 633.

6. *Ibid.*, p. 655.

7. Solve, *Stuart Politics in Chapman's "Tragedy of Chabot,"* p. 62.

8. *Journal of English and Germanic Philology,* XXIX (1930), 303.

9. *Ibid.*, p. 304.

10. Parrott's demonstration that Chapman could have had no part in *The Ball,* even though his name appears on the title page, removes the possibility of a similar lapse between any two of the comedies. See Parrott, *Comedies,* pp. 869-75.

11. Parrott, *Tragedies,* p. 631.

12. *Chabot,* I, 1, 20-22.

13. *Byron's Conspiracy,* "Prologus," ll. 23-24.

14. *Chabot,* I, 1, 76-80. (Italics mine.)

15. Bartlett, *The Poems of George Chapman,* p. 228, ll. 1-2.

16. *Ibid.*, p. 229, ll. 39-42.

17. *Ibid.*, pp. 236-37, ll. 1-8.

18. *Ibid.*, p. 447.

19. *Ibid.*, p. 449.

20. *Chabot,* I, 1, 30.

21. *Bussy D'Ambois,* V, 2, 1-53.

22. *Chabot,* I, 1, 26-27.

23. ll. 184-85.

24. ll. 102-07.

25. II, 3, 123-28.

26. IV, 1, 77-78.

27. ll. 137-40.

28. ll. 288-92. The King states in an earlier soliloquy that he is glad the Admiral's boldness has been condemned:

that I may pardon . . .
For I could never find him obstinate
In any mind he held, when once he saw
Th' error with which he laboured.

IV, 1, 167, 172-174.

29. II, 2, 53-57. Note also these lines of Montmorency that re-
flect the mental state of one whose life Reason does not control:
And 'tis my misery to be plac'd in such
A sphere, where I am whirl'd by violence
Of a fierce raging motion, and not what
My own will would incline me.

III, 1, 221-24.

30. l. 58.

31. *The Revenge of Bussy D'Ambois,* IV, 1, 12-13.

32. The advice of Chabot's father-in-law to the Queen clearly
illustrates the kind of passion that men must refuse to tolerate:

There's nothing
Doth more eclipse the honours of our soul
Than an ill-grounded and ill-followed passion.

Chabot, III, 1, 102-04

33. II, 2, 64.

34. IV, 1, 382-84.

35. V, 1, 26.

36. *Bussy D'Ambois,* V, 4, 94.

37. *Byron's Tragedy,* V, 4, 51-55.

38. *The Revenge of Bussy D'Ambois,* V, 5, 175-92.

39. *Chabot,* V, 1, 26-32.

40. Perhaps the result of Shirley's rewriting.

41. V, 3, 160-202. Parrott believes (*Tragedies,* p. 648) that
there is "a substratum of Chapman in this scene, but it is heavily
overlaid with Shirley."

42. ll. 192-94.
43. Cicero, *De Officiis*, p. 97.
44. Seneca, III, 19.
45. *Chabot*, II, 2, 78-79.
46. I, 1, 48-57.
47. I, 2, 107-13.
48. II, 3, 14-16.
49. l. 78.
50. ll. 79-81.
51. ll. 160-61.
52. Parrott, *Tragedies*, p. 643.
53. *Chabot*, III, 1, 97-104.
54. ll. 140-45.
55. Parrott, *Tragedies*, p. 633.
56. *The Revenge of Bussy D'Ambois*, IV, 3, 41-49.
57. *Chabot*, IV, 1, 235.
58. ll. 419-20.
59. V, 3, 174-77.
60. I, 2, 70-73.
61. V, 2, 161-62.
62. I, 1, 11-12.
63. ll. 86-88.
64. V, 1, 80.
65. ll. 92-94.
66. V, 3, 193.

CHAPTER FIVE

1. Parrott, *Tragedies*, p. 655.
2. *Ibid.*
3. *The Tragedy of Caesar and Pompey*, p. 343.
4. Parrott states (*Tragedies*, p. 657) that the sources for this

tragedy "are in the main three of Plutarch's *Lives,* those of Caesar, Pompey, and Cato Minor. In addition Kern shows that Chapman made repeated drafts upon one of his favourite books, Plutarch's *Morals."*

5. *Caesar and Pompey,* I, 1, 3-6.

6. Parrott, acknowledging that Chapman "had before him models by the greatest playwrights of the age—Shakespeare, *Julius Caesar* 1601, *Antony and Cleopatra* 1607-8, *Coriolanus* 1609, and Ben Jonson *Sejanus,* 1603, and *Catiline,* 1611," nevertheless believes that it is plain that Chapman, "with his usual independence of attitude, disregarded the work of his contemporaries, and struck out along lines more congenial to his peculiar temperament." *Tragedies,* p. 657.

7. *Caesar and Pompey,* I, 1, 24-28.

8. I, 2, 87-90.

9. ll. 117-20.

10. l. 37.

11. ll. 221-26.

12. l. 167.

13. II, 3, 10. Shakespeare in his *Julius Caesar* and later Barrie in his *Dear Brutus* both adopted the Stoic idea that the "fault" lay in the individual, not in Fortune. See *Julius Caesar,* I, 2, 137-39:

> Men at some times are masters of their fates:
> The fault, dear Brutus, is not in our stars,
> But in ourselves, that we are underlings.

See also *Dear Brutus,* p. 111.

14. ll. 74-81.

15. It should not be inferred, however, that the Stoics excluded divination from their philosophy. For although, as Zeller points out, "In a system so purely based on nature as theirs, the supposi-

tion that God works for definite ends after the manner of men, exceptionally announcing to one or the other a definite result—in short, the marvellous—was out of place" (*The Stoics, Epicureans, and Sceptics,* p. 371), the Stoics, nevertheless, regarded the power of divination as a gift which the gods could not refuse to grant to men. For a full discussion of this aspect of Stoic dogma, see *ibid.,* pp. 370-80.

16. *Caesar and Pompey,* II, 5, 12-17.
17. ll. 17-21.
18. III, 2, 114-16.
19. Parrott, *Tragedies,* p. 659.
20. *Caesar and Pompey,* I, 2, 113.
21. IV, 4, 1-3.
22. V, 2, 205-09.
23. l. 188.
24. I, 1, 1-6.
25. l, 2, 142-43.
26. ll. 178-82.
27. ll. 265-69.
28. III, 1, 1.
29. ll. 22-27.
30. ll. 28-29.
31. ll. 30-31.
32. *The Odysseys of Homer,* trans. George Chapman, ed. Richard Hooper, Vol. II, Bk. 24, l. 38.
33. *Caesar and Pompey,* III, 1, 32.
34. l. 35.
35. l. 37.
36. l. 39.
37. l. 40.
38. l. 41.
39. l. 42.

40. IV, i, *passim.*

41. ll. 10-11.

42. ll. 45-46, 51-52.

43. Parrott, *Tragedies,* p. 671, note to IV, i.

44. *Caesar and Pompey,* IV, 3, 40-44.

45. ll. 56-58.

46. ll. 69-75.

47. ll. 82-84.

48. ll. 90-92.

49. Parrott, *Tragedies,* p. 672, note to IV, 3.

50. In his note on this scene, Parrott comments: "He [Chapman] has totally transformed the character of Cornelia. Instead of the passionate emotional woman, swooning at the sight of her husband and breaking out into wild lamentations, as is recorded by Lucan, *Pharsalia,* VIII, 50-108, and Plutarch, *Pompey,* 74, he has made her a *philosophress,* l. 147, of the Stoic school, and a fit match for Pompey, as Chapman pictures him in the latter part of this play." *Ibid.,* p. 674.

51. *Ibid.,* p. 675, note to V, 1, 80-162.

52. *Caesar and Pompey,* V, 1, 152.

53. ll. 153-54.

54. l. 155.

55. l. 25.

56. ll. 162-64.

57. ll. 178-79.

58. ll. 181-82.

59. Epictetus, *Discourses,* p. 449: "If you wish for reason, you must let outward things go."

60. *Caesar and Pompey,* V, 1, 185-86.

61. ll. 202-07.

62. ll. 208-13.

63. ll. 227-32.

64. *Byron's Tragedy,* I, 1, 141-44:

> Let him by virtue quite [cut] off from Fortune
> Her feather'd shoulders and her winged shoes,
> And thrust from her light feet her turning stone
> That she may ever tarry by his throne.

Parrott also calls attention, p. 611, note to I, 1, 141-44, to the similarity of the two passages.

65. *Caesar and Pompey,* V, 1, 250-51.

66. I, 2, 21: "He will be stoical."

67. Algernon Charles Swinburne, *Contemporaries of Shakespeare,* ed. Edmund Gosse, p. 95.

68. *Caesar and Pompey,* I, 1, 57-61.

69. ll. 83-84.

70. I, 2, 10.

71. ll, 4, 5-6.

72. ll. 55-57.

73. l. 62.

74. Cicero, *De Officiis,* p. 115.

75. *Caesar and Pompey,* IV, 5, 8-10.

76. ll. 27-31, 43-44.

77. Statilius is listed in the *Dramatis Personae* as *"a disciple of Cato."*

78. IV, 5, 47-51.

79. l. 53.

80. ll. 57-59.

81. ll. 63-66.

82. ll. 71-72.

83. ll. 72-79.

84. ll. 80-83.

85. Parrott, *Tragedies,* p. 673, note to IV, 5, 45.

86. *Caesar and Pompey,* IV, 5, 90.

87. Parrott, *Tragedies,* p. 673.

88. *Ibid.*, p. 78.
89. *Caesar and Pompey*, IV, 5, 97.
90. Epictetus, *Manual*, trans. Sanford, p. 21v.
91. *Caesar and Pompey*, IV, 5, 107-10.
92. l. 141.
93. ll. 143-45.
94. ll. 150-55.
95. V, 2, 9.
96. ll. 10-18.
97. ll. 106-13.
98. ll. 134-43; compare with passage cited in note n. 88.
99. l. 177.
100. Parrott, *Tragedies*, p. 341.
101. *Ibid.*, pp. 656-57.
102. Spencer, *Death and Elizabethan Tragedy*, p. 175.
103. *Ibid.*, pp. 176, 179.
104. Roy W. Battenhouse, "Chapman and the Nature of Man," *English Literary History*, XII, No. 2 (1945), 96.

EPILOGUE

1. Gotthold Ephraim Lessing, *Laokoon*, ed. A. Hamann, p. 12: "Alles Stoische ist untheatralisch."

APPENDIX A

1. Parrott, *Tragedies*, p. 692.
2. *Ibid.*, p. 690.
3. *Ibid.*, pp. 690-91.
4. *Ibid.*, p. 691.
5. H. Dugdale Sykes, "Peele's *'Alphonsus, Emperor of Germany,'*" *Sidelights on Elizabethan Drama* ([England], 1924), p. 79.

6. *Ibid.*

7. *Ibid.*

8. Harold M. Dowling, "Peele and Some Doubtful Plays," *Notes and Queries,* CLXIV (1933), 366.

9. *Ibid.,* p. 367.

10. Fredson Thayer Bowers, *"Alphonsus, Emperor of Germany,* and the *Ur-Hamlet," Modern Language Notes,* XLVIII (1933), 101-02.

APPENDIX B

1. Parrott, *Tragedies,* p. 717.

2. *Ibid.,* p. 719-20.

3. H. Dugdale Sykes, " *'Revenge for Honour':* Glapthorne's Play Attributed to Chapman," *Notes and Queries,* Twelfth Series, I (1916), 402.

4. J. H. Walter, *"Revenge for Honour:* 'Date, Authorship, and Sources,' " *Review of English Studies,* XIII (1937), 436.

5. Chester Linn Shaver, "The Date of *Revenge for Honour," Modern Language Notes,* LIII (1938), 98.

6. Parrott, *Tragedies,* p. 713.

7. *Revenge for Honour,* I, 1, 286-89. See Parrott, *Tragedies.*

8. ll. 326-30, 333-36.

9. III, 2, 145-47.

10. IV, 1, 118-19.

11. V, 2, 341.

APPENDIX C

1. Franck L. Schoell, *Études sur l'Humanisme Continental en Angleterre à la Fin de la Renaissance.*

2. Published under the title: *Epicteti Enchiridion, hoc est pugio, siue ars humanae vitae correctrix, una cum Cebetis Thebani Tabula,*

qua vitae humanae prudenter instituendae ratio continetur, Graece et Latine, quibus tum demum accesserunt, e graeco translata, Simplicii . . . *scholia, Arriani Commentariorum de Epicteti disputationibus libri IIII, item alia eiusdem argumenti.*

3. *The Manuell of Epictetus. Translated out of Greeke into French, and now into English, conferred with two Latine translations; hereunto are annexed Annotations, and also the Apothegs of the same author. By Ia. Sanford. Imprinted at London by H. Bynneman for Leonard Maylard. Anno. 1567.* (Microfilm available in the Columbia University Library.)

4. Bartlett, *op. cit.*, p. 448, note to *"A great Man."*

5. For this and following similar items, the reader should consult the STC.

6. *The Stoic and Epicurean Philosophers,* the Complete Extant Writings of Epicurus, Epictetus, Lucretius, Marcus Aurelius, ed. Whitney J. Oates.

7. Schoell, *Études sur l'Humanisme Continental en Angleterre à la Fin de la Renaissance,* p. 74.

8. *Ibid.,* pp. 43-61.

BIBLIOGRAPHY

Alston, Leonard. Stoic and Christian in the Second Century. A comparison of the ethical teaching of Marcus Aurelius with that of contemporary and antecedent Christianity. London, Longmans, Green, 1906.

Anderson, Ruth Leila. Elizabethan Psychology and Shakespeare's Plays. University of Iowa Humanistic Studies, III, No. 4. Iowa City, 1927.

Archer, William. The Old Drama and the New; an Essay in Revaluation. Boston, Small Maynard, 1923.

Arnold, Matthew. "An Essay on Marcus Aurelius," The Stoic and Epicurean Philosophers. Ed. with an Introduction by Whitney J. Oates. New York, Random House, 1940. Pp. 593-610.

——Essays Literary and Critical. With an Introduction by G. K. Chesterton. Chapters X, XI, XII. New York, Dutton [reprinted], 1914.

Aurelius, Marcus. "The Meditations of Marcus Aurelius." Trans. by G. Long. The Stoic and Epicurean Philosophers. The complete extant writings of Epicurus, Epictetus, Lucretius, Marcus Aurelius. Ed. with an Introduction by Whitney J. Oates. New York, Random House, 1940. Pp. 491-585.

Ayers, Harry Morgan. "Chapman's Homer and Others," The Nation, CIV (1917), 439-41.

Baker, Howard. Induction to Tragedy. A study in a development of form in Gorboduc, The Spanish Tragedy, and Titus Andronicus. Baton Rouge, Louisiana State University Press, 1939.

Baldwin, William. A Treatise of Morall Phylosophie. Contaynyng the sayinges of the wyse. 2 parts. Gathered and Englyshed by William Baldwin. London, 1547. Microfilm in Columbia University Library.

Barrie, J. M. Dear Brutus. A comedy in three acts. New York, Scribner, 1922.

Bartlett, Phyllis B. "Chapman's Revisions in his 'Iliads,' " *A Journal of English Literary History*, II (1935), 92-119.

——"The Heroes of Chapman's Homer," *Review of English Studies*, XVII (1941), 257-80.

Battenhouse, Roy W. "Chapman and the Nature of Man," *A Journal of English Literary History*, XII, No. 2 (1945), 87-107.

——"Chapman's 'The Shadow of Night': An Interpretation," *Studies in Philology*, XXXVII (1941), 504-608.

Bevan, Edwyn. Stoics and Sceptics. Oxford, Clarendon Press, 1913.

Boas, Frederick S. "The Source of Chapman's 'The Conspiracie and Tragedy of Charles, Duke of Byron' and 'The Revenge of Bussy D'Ambois,' " *Athenaeum* (1903), pp. 51-52.

Bowers, Frederick Thayer. " 'Alphonsus, Emperor of Germany,' and the 'Ur-Hamlet,' " *Modern Language Notes*, XLVIII (1933), 101-08.

——"The Date and Composition of 'Alphonsus, Emperor of Germany,' " *Harvard Studies and Notes in Philology and Literature*, XV-XVII (1933), 165-89.

——"The Date of 'Revenge for Honour,' " *Modern Language Notes*, LII (1937), 192-96.

Bradbrook, M. C. Themes and Conventions of Elizabethan Tragedy. Cambridge, University Press, 1935.

——The School of Night, a Study in the Literary Relationships of Sir Walter Raleigh. Cambridge, University Press, 1936.

Bradley, A. C. Shakespearean Tragedy, Lectures on *Hamlet, Othello, King Lear, Macbeth*. London, Macmillan, 1926.

Breton, Nicholas. Melancholy Humours. Ed., with "An Essay on Elizabethan Melancholy," by G. B. Harrison. London, Scholartis Press, 1929.

Brooke, Tucker. The Tudor Drama, Cambridge [Mass.], Houghton Mifflin, 1911.

Bruno, Giordano. The Heroic Enthusiasts. An ethical poem. Trans. by L. Williams. Two parts, part the first, London, George Redway, 1887; part the second, London, Bernard Quaritch, 1889.

Buckley, George T. Atheism in the English Renaissance. Chicago, University of Chicago Press, 1932.

Bullen, A. H. "George Chapman," Elizabethans. London, Chapman and Hall, 1924. Pp. 49-69.

Bush, Douglas. Mythology and the Renaissance Tradition in English Poetry. Minneapolis, University of Minnesota Press, 1932.

——The Renaissance and English Humanism. Canada, University of Toronto Press, 1939.

Campbell, Lily B. Shakespeare's Tragic Heroes: Slaves of Passion. Cambridge, University Press, 1930.

Chapman, George. Bussy D'Ambois and The Revenge of Bussy D'Ambois, by George Chapman. Ed. Frederick S. Boas. Boston, Heath, 1905.

——The Iliads of Homer. Prince of Poets, never before in any language truly translated, with a comment on some of his chief places. Done according to the Greek by George Chapman, with Introduction and Notes, by the Rev. Richard Hooper. 2 vols., 2d ed. London, John Russell Smith, 1865.

——The Odysseys of Homer. Translated according to the Greek by George Chapman, with Introduction and Notes by Richard Hooper. 2 vols. London, John Russell Smith, 1857.

——The Poems of George Chapman. Ed. Phyllis Brooks Bartlett. Modern Language Association, Menasha, Wis., Banta, 1941.

——The Comedies of George Chapman. Ed. with Introduction and Notes by Thomas Marc Parrott. New York, Dutton, 1914.

——The Tragedies of George Chapman. Ed. with Introduction and Notes by Thomas Marc Parrott. New York, Dutton, 1910.

——The Tragedie of Chabot Admiral of France. Written by George Chapman and James Shirley. Reprinted from Quarto of 1639. Ed. with an Introduction and Notes by Ezra Lehman. Publications of the University of Pennsylvania, Series in Philology and Literature, X. Philadelphia, Winston, 1906.

Cicero. De Officiis. With an English translation by Walter Miller. The Loeb Classical Library. London, Macmillan, 1913.

De Senectute, De Amicitia, De Divinatione. With an English translation by William Armstead Falconer. The Loeb Classical Library. London, Putnam, 1923.

Coleridge, S. T. Coleridge's Miscellaneous Criticism. Ed. Thomas Middleton Raysor. London, Constable, 1936. Pp. 231-34.

Craig, Hardin. "Ethics in the Jacobean Drama: the Case of Chapman," Essays in Dramatic Literature. The Parrott Presentation Volume, by pupils of Professor Thomas Marc Parrott of Princeton University, published in his honor. Ed. Hardin Craig. Princeton, Princeton University Press, 1935. Pp. 25-46.

——The Enchanted Glass, the Elizabethan Mind in Literature. New York, Oxford University Press, 1936.

Creizenach, William. The English Drama in the Age of Shakespeare. Trans. from "Geschicte des neueren Dramas." Philadelphia, Lippincott, 1916.

Cunliffe, J. W. The Influence of Seneca on Elizabethan Tragedy. London, Macmillan, 1893.

Curry, Walter Clyde. Shakespeare's Philosophical Patterns. Baton Rouge, Louisiana State University Press, 1937.

Davidson, William L. The Stoic Creed. Edinburgh, Clark, 1907.

Dobell, Bertram. "Newly Discovered Documents of the Elizabethan and Jacobean Periods," *Athanaeum* (1901), pp. 369-70, 403-04, 433-34, 465-67.

Dowling, Harold M. "Peele and Some Doubtful Plays," *Notes and Queries,* CLXIV (1933), 366-67.

Dryden, John. Essays of John Dryden. Selected and ed. W. P. Ker. 2 vols. Oxford, Clarendon Press, 1926.

Dunn, Esther Cloudman. The Literature of Shakespeare's England. New York, Scribner, 1936.

DuVair, Guillaume. The Moral Philosophie of The Stoicks. Written originally in French, and englished for the benefit of them which are ignorant of that tongue by Th. Iames, Fellow of New College in Oxford. London, 1598. Microfilm in Columbia University Library.

Eliot, T. S. "Four English Dramatists," Elizabethan Essays. London, Faber & Faber, 1934.

——John Dryden, the Poet, the Dramatist, the Critic. Three Essays. New York, Elsa Holliday, 1932.

——"Seneca in Elizabethan Translation," "Shakespeare and the Stoicism of Seneca," and "The Metaphysical Poets," Selected Essays. New York, Harcourt, Brace, 1932.

——The Sacred Wood, Essays on Poetry and Criticism. 3d ed. London, Methuen, 1932.

Ellis, Havelock. Chapman. With illustrative passages. Bloomsbury, The Nonesuch Press, 1934.

Ellis-Fermor, U. M. The Jacobean Drama; an Interpretation. London, Methuen, 1936.

Epictetus. The Manuell of Epictetus. Translated out of Greek into French, and now into English, conferred with two Latine translations; hereto are annexed Annotations, and also the Apothegs of the same author. By Ia. Sanford. Imprinted at London by H. Bynneman for Leonard Maylard. Anno. 1567. Microfilm in Columbia University Library.

——Epictetus His Manuall and Cebes His Table. Out of the Greeke originall, by Io. Healey. At London, Printed for Th. Thorpe, 1610.

——"The Discourses of Epictetus, Fragments, and The Manual of

Epictetus," trans. by P. E. Matheson. The Stoic and Epicurean Philosophers. The complete extant writings of Epicurus, Epictetus, Lucretius, Marcus Aurelius. Ed. with an Introduction by Whitney J. Oates. New York, Random House, 1940. Pp. 223-484.

Erasmus. Proverbes or Adagies. With newe addicions gathered out of the Chiliades of Erasmus by Richard Tauener. Imprinted at Lõdon in Fletstrete at the sygne of the Whyte Harte, 1539.

Farnham, Willard. The Medieval Heritage of Elizabethan Tragedy. Berkeley, University of California Press, 1936.

Ferguson, A. S. "The Plays of George Chapman," *Modern Language Review,* XIII (1918), 1-24.

Froude, James Anthony. Thomas Carlyle, a History of the First Forty Years of His Life, 1795-1835. Two volumes in one. New York, Ogilivie, [n. d.].

Gilbert, Alan H. "Chapman's Fortune with Winged Hands," *Modern Language Notes,* LII (1937), 190-92.

Grierson, H. J. C. Cross Currents in English Literature of the XVIIth Century. London, Chatto & Windus, 1929.

Hazlitt, William. "On Marston, Chapman, Decker, and Webster," Lecture III of Lectures on the Age of Elizabeth, the Complete Works of William Hazlitt. Centenary edition, ed. P. P. Howe, after the edition of A. R. Waller and Arnold Glover. 21 vols. VI (London, Dent, 1931). Pp. 230-34.

Hudson, William Henry. The Story of the Renaissance. London, Cassell, 1912.

Hughes, Merritt Y. "Review" of H. B. Lathrop's Translations from the Classics into English from Caxton to Chapman, 1477-1620, *Modern Language Notes,* L (1935), 195-98.

Irwin, William Robert. The Making of Jonathan Wild; a Study in the Literary Method of Henry Fielding. New York, Columbia University Press, 1941. Pp. 43-79.

Kennedy, Charles W. "Political Theory in the Plays of George Chapman," Essays in Dramatic Literature. The Parrott Presentation Volume (see first entry under Hardin Craig). Princeton, Princeton University Press, 1935. Pp. 73-86.

Kern, Adolf. George Chapman's Tragodie "Caesar and Pompey" und ihre Quellen. Halle a. S., Buchdruckerei von H. John, 1901.

Kreider, Paul V. Elizabethan Comic Character Conventions as Revealed in the Comedies of George Chapman. University of Michigan Publications, Language and Literature, XVII. Ann Arbor, University of Michigan Press, 1935.

Kristeller, Paul O. The Philosophy of Marsilio Ficino. Trans. into English by Virginia Conant. New York, Columbia University Press, 1943.

——and John H. Randall, Jr. "The Study of Renaissance Philosophies," Journal of the History of Ideas, II (1941), 449-96.

Lamb, Charles. Specimens of English Dramatic Poets, Who Lived about the Time of Shakespeare. With Notes, new ed., complete in one volume. New York, Putnam, 1850.

Lathrop, Henry Burrowes. Translations from the Classics into English from Caxton to Chapman, 1477-1620. University of Wisconsin Studies in Language and Literature, No. 35. Madison, University of Wisconsin Press, 1933.

Lessing, Gotthold Ephraim. Laokoon, in German Classics. Ed. with English Notes, by A. Hamann. Oxford, Clarendon Press, 1878.

Lewis, Wyndham. The Lion and The Fox; the Role of the Hero in the Plays of Shakespeare. New York, Harper, 1927.

Lipsius, Justus. Tvvo Bookes of Constancie. Written in Latine by Justus Lipsius; Englished by Sir John Stradling, ed. with an Introduction by Rudolf Kirk, Notes by Clayton Morris Hall. New Brunswick, N. J., Rutgers University Press, 1939.

Lodge, Thomas. The Workes of Lvcivs Annaevs Seneca. Newly inlarged and corrected by Thomas Lodge. London, 1620.

Lowell, James Russell. "Chapman," The Old English Dramatists, Cambridge, Mass., Houghton Mifflin, 1922. Pp. 78-99.

Lovejoy, Arthur Oncken and George Boas. A Documentary History of Primitivism and Related Ideas. With supplementary essays by W. F. Albright and P. E. Dumont; Appendix: "Some Meanings of Nature." Baltimore, The Johns Hopkins Press, 1935. Pp. 447-56.

Lucas, F. L. Seneca and Elizabethan Tragedy. Cambridge, The University Press, 1922.

Matthews, Brander. A Study of the Drama. Boston, Houghton Mifflin, 1910.

Matthiesen, F. O. Translations, an Elizabethan Art. Cambridge, Mass., Harvard University Press, 1931.

Meyer, Edward. Machiavelli and the Elizabethan Drama. Weimar, Felber, 1897.

Mills, Laurens J. One Soul in Bodies Twain; Friendship in Tudor Literature and Stuart Drama. Bloomington, Ind., Principia Press, 1937.

Morgan, Roberta. "Some Stoic Lines in 'Hamlet' and the Problem of Interpretation," Philological Quarterly, XX (1941), 549-58.

Morrow, Constance. The Effect of Astronomical Ideas in Sixteenth Century England on Chapman and Marlowe. Master's thesis. Columbia University, February, 1938.

Nicoll, Allardyce. British Drama, an Historical Survey from the Beginnings to the Present Time. London, Harrap, 1925.

Oakesmith, John. The Religion of Plutarch; a Pagan Creed of Apostolic Times, an Essay. London, Longmans, 1902.

Parrott, Thomas Marc. Review of N. D. Solve's "Stuart Politics in Chapman's Tragedy of Chabot," The Journal of English and Germanic Philology, XXIX (1930), 300-04.

——and Robert Hamilton Ball. A Short View of Elizabethan

Drama. Together with some account of its principal playwrights and the conditions under which it was produced. New York, Scribner, 1943.

Patch, Howard Rollins. The Tradition of the Goddess Fortuna in Medieval Philosophy and Literature. Smith College Series in Modern Languages, III, No. 4. Northampton, Mass., Smith College, 1922.

Perkinson, Richard H. "Nature and the Tragic Hero in Chapman's Bussy Plays," Modern Language Quarterly, III (1942), 263-85.

Phelps, William Lyon. George Chapman. The Best Plays of the Old Dramatists, ed. with an Introduction and Notes. New York, Scribner, 1895.

Plutarch. Plutarch's Moralia. With an English translation by Frank Cole Babbitt. 14 vols. Loeb Classical Library. London and New York, Putnam, 1927-39.

Pogrell, Nancy von. Die Philosophisch-poetische Entwicklung George Chapmans; ein versuch zur interpretation seines Werkes, Britannica, XVIII. Hamburg, Friedericksen, de Gruyter, 1939.

Read, Herbert. "The Nature of Metaphysical Poetry," Criterion, I (Oct. 1922—July 1923), 246-65.

Rutledge, Leslie A. George Chapman's Theory of the Soul and of Poetry. An unpublished Harvard University doctoral thesis, March, 1938.

Schelling, Felix E. "Ben Jonson and the Classical School," Publication of the Modern Language Association of America, XIII (1898), 221-49.

Schoell, Franck L. Études sur L'Humanisme Continental en Angleterre à la fin de la Renaissance. Paris, Champion, 1926.

——"George Chapman's 'Commonplace Book,'" Modern Philology, XVII (1919-20), 199-218.

——"George Chapman and the Italian Neo-Latinists of the Quattrocento," Modern Philology, XIII (1915), 215-38.

Seneca. Ad Lucilium Epistulae Morales. With an English translation by Richard M. Gummere. 3 vols. Loeb Classical Library.
London, Putnam, 1917-25.

Shakespeare, William. "The Tragedy of Julius Caesar," The
Works of Shakespeare. Ed. by Michael MacMillan. London,
Methuen, 1902.

Shaver, Chester Linn. "The Date of Revenge for Honour," Modern Language Notes, LIII (1938), 96-98.

Simpson, Percy. The Theme of Revenge in Elizabethan Tragedy.
Annual Shakespeare lecture of the British Academy, from the
Proceedings of the British Academy, XXI. London, Humphrey
Milford, 1935.

Smalley, Donald. "The Ethical Bias of Chapman's Homer,"
Studies in Philology, XXXVI (1939), 169-91.

Smith, James. "George Chapman," Scrutiny, III (1934-35),
339-50; IV (1935-36), 45-61.

Solve, Norma Dobie. Stuart Politics in Chapman's "Tragedy of
Chabot." University of Michigan Publications, Language and
Literature, IV. Ann Arbor, University of Michigan, 1928.

Sonnenschein, E. A. "Stoicism in English Literature," Contemporary Review, CXXIV (1923), 355-65.

Spencer, Theodore. Death and Elizabethan Tragedy, a Study of
Convention and Opinion in the Elizabethan Drama. Cambridge,
Harvard University Press, 1936.

Spens, Janet. "Chapman's Ethical Thought," Essays and Studies,
XI (1925), 145-69.

Stock, St. George. Stoicism. London, Constable, 1908.

Swinburne, Algernon Charles. "George Chapman," Contemporaries of Shakespeare. Ed. Edmund Gosse and Thomas James
Wise. London, William Heinemann, 1919. Pp. 15-142.

——Essay on the Poetical and Dramatic Works of G. Chapman.
London, Chatto & Windus, 1875.

——Letters on the Works of George Chapman. With a Prefatory Note by Edmund Gosse. London, printed for private circulation, 1909. Microfilm in Columbia University Library.

——"George Chapman," The Age of Shakespeare, New York, Harper, 1908. Pp. 255-61.

Sykes, H. Dugdale. "Peele's 'Alphonsus, Emperor of Germany,' " Sidelights on Elizabethan Drama. England, Oxford University Press, 1924, pp. 79-98.

——" 'Revenge for Honour': Glapthorne's Play Attributed to Chapman," *Notes and Queries,* Twelfth Series, I (1916), 401-04.

Tannenbaum, Samuel A. Elizabethan Bibliographies, number 5, "George Chapman (A Concise Bibliography)." New York, 1938.

Thomas, D. L. "Authorship of 'Revenge for Honour,' " *Modern Philology,* V (1907-08), 617-36.

Thorndike, Ashley H. Tragedy. Boston, Houghton Mifflin, 1908.

Walter, J. H. "Revenge for Honour: Date, Authorship and Sources," *Review of English Studies,* XIII (1937), 435-37.

Wells, Henry W. Elizabethan and Jacobean Playwrights. New York, Columbia University Press, 1939.

Wenley, R. M. Stoicism and Its Influence. Boston, Marshall Jones, 1924.

Wilson, Harold S. "Some Meanings of Nature in Renaissance Literature," *Journal of the History of Ideas,* II (1941), 430-48.

Worthington, Jane. Wordsworth's Reading of Roman Prose. Yale Studies in English, CII. New Haven, Yale University Press, 1946.

Zanta, Leontine. La Renaissance du Stoïcisme au XVI Siécle. Paris, H. Champion, 1914.

Zeller, Eduard. The Stoics, Epicureans and Sceptics. Trans. from the German by Rev. Oswald J. Reichel. New and rev. ed. London, Longmans, Green, 1892.

INDEX